T0352330

Shell Shock in France

1914–18

Shell Shock in France

1914—18

Based on a War Diary
kept by

CHARLES S. MYERS, C.B.E., F.R.S.

Temporary Lieutenant-Colonel, Royal Army Medical Corps
Sometime Consulting Psychologist to the
British Armies in France

CAMBRIDGE
AT THE UNIVERSITY PRESS
1940

CAMBRIDGE UNIVERSITY PRESS
Cambridge, New York, Melbourne, Madrid, Cape Town,
Singapore, São Paulo, Delhi, Tokyo, Mexico City

Cambridge University Press
The Edinburgh Building, Cambridge CB2 8RU, UK

Published in the United States of America by
Cambridge University Press, New York

www.cambridge.org
Information on this title: www.cambridge.org/9781107673786

First published 1940
First paperback edition 2011

A catalogue record for this publication is available from the British Library

ISBN 978-1-107-67378-6 Paperback

To

MY WIFE

CONTENTS

PREFACE

The title of this book is not strictly accurate; but it is the best within a small compass that I could devise. In it not only have I tried to give some account of the psycho-neuroses collectively known as 'shell shock' in the last war, their nature and treatment and the disposal of such cases: I have also examined their relation to 'shell concussion', and I have described the disposal of the psychotic cases (the 'insanities'), with all of which I was concerned from 1915 to 1917 in France. I have further added some account of the continuation of my work in Great Britain on my return from France at the end of 1917 until after the end of the war.

It is so long since any book has been written on so-called 'shell shock' that the present volume may well serve to re-enlighten members of the general public as to its nature, and to convince them how dependent it is on a previous psycho-neurotic history and inherited predisposition, on inadequate examination and selection of soldiers fitted for the Front Line, and on the lack of proper discipline and *esprit de corps*; and how necessary it may be to adopt apparently harsh measures in order to diminish the undoubted 'contagiousness' and the needless prolongation of the complaint.

The personal experiences which I have narrated may perhaps raise a doubt in some minds as to how far the present senior administrative Officers of the Army Medical Service and the Adjutant-General's Department will be prevented from repeating the same mistakes—errors of commission, omission, and especially of wasteful procrastination—as arose during the last war. But some of these errors, it must be realized, were excusably due to the notorious lack of training of the past generation of physicians in mental disorders and to the then unprecedented conditions of warfare, e.g. the strain of immobile trench fighting, the preponderance of inexperienced, quickly trained, non-professional soldiers, etc.

For my part, I am hopeful that, if it comes to their notice, the book will exercise some guiding influence upon them; and I believe that it will be of assistance to the younger members of the Royal Army Medical Corps who, with the advancement of medical science, and of psychological medicine in particular, will have received a more liberal and effective education than their forbears—especially to those who are directly concerned with the treatment and disposal of 'nervous' and 'mental' cases in warfare.

This book is a record of personal experiences. I have, however, omitted, because it seemed to me unwise and useless, to mention certain exceptional personal difficulties with which I was confronted in one quarter in France. I prefer, after all these years, rather to recall the outstanding sympathy, help and courtesy which I received from, and the valued friendships which I formed with, the abler, more enlightened and more progressive members of the Army Medical Service both in France and in this country, nursing the belief that such Officers are considerably more numerous to-day than they were a quarter of a century ago.

C. S. M.

January 1940

Chapter I

THE ORIGIN AND DEVELOPMENT
OF MY WORK IN FRANCE

THE OUTBREAK OF THE WAR

AT the beginning of August 1914 I returned to England from a climbing holiday in Switzerland on the very eve of the outbreak of war. When I reached Paris, I found the city in a state of great excitement and turmoil. Outside the offices of the chief banks long queues of French people were drawn up, waiting to withdraw their money. The manager of my hotel, at which I was known, accepted my cheque only when I made it clear to him that I had no money with me for the payment of my bill. At the Gare du Nord, the conductor of the restaurant-car in the train proceeding to Calais refused admission to any passengers who could not pay for their luncheons in gold or silver; he would not even accept French notes in settlement of the restaurant account.

On arriving at Cambridge, I resumed the work in my psychological laboratory on which I had been previously engaged—the analysis of primitive Australian music from a unique series of phonographic records that had been collected and recently presented to the University by the late Prof. Baldwin Spencer of the University of Adelaide. But amid the general preparations for warfare, the exciting news and the atmosphere of constant rumours, such research became each day more difficult. I tried in vain to concentrate my attention on it; but the feeling of its incongruity and unimportance increased to such an extent that by the end of August I could work at it no longer, and decided to seek medical work in the field, in France.

First I approached the War Office, where, although my application was entered and I underwent a medical examination, I was politely informed that no doctors over forty years of age (I was then in my forty-second year) were being accepted for service abroad. I tried next the Order of the Hospital of St John of Jerusalem and the British Red Cross Society, then working independently of one another. The former sent me an offer of work in France several months after I had left England. At the latter the eminent surgeon in charge was good enough to hint to me that, as so many applications were being received in excess of the number of posts available, social influence alone could procure me success. I turned then to the French Red Cross Society, which soon sent me an offer of medical work at a small French railway station where I would have two dressers and two untrained nurses to assist me. But a few minutes after the receipt of this letter, a telegram arrived cancelling the offer as it had been accepted by some other doctor. By chance, I read in my old Hospital Journal that the Duchess of Westminster had just taken out a hospital unit to France, staffed by physicians, surgeons and nurses trained at St Bartholomew's Hospital, whose names were announced, and among whom I recognized several old acquaintances and one or two who had formerly 'clerked' under me in the wards at Bart.'s when I was house-physician there. I decided to cross in mufti to Paris where, I understood, this unit was temporarily housed in a hotel, awaiting the allocation of a site for its work. I applied for the necessary passport from the Foreign Office and obtained it without difficulty.

IN PARIS

On 17 October 1914 I left Victoria station at 10 a.m., crossing from Folkestone to Dieppe by a small steamer, the *Arundel*, and reached Paris at 9.50 p.m. The passengers were mostly French people returning to Paris after their initial panic. In the train from Dieppe to Paris I entered into conversation with a Parisian *commerçant*, who described the utter insufficiency of the present surgical work at Dieppe, offering me his house there and the use of his cars for my wife and family if I would only return to Dieppe and give help

there. On the following morning I visited the
hotel where the Duchess of Westminster's Hospital Unit had been already waiting for sixteen
days, discussed the situation with some of my
friends, and took a room at their hotel. The next
day I met the Duchess, who promised to do what
she could for me. Three days later I was definitely
given a promise of work in the hospital whenever
it should be opened, and accordingly I ordered a
nondescript khaki uniform at the shop of a Paris
tailor.

AT LE TOUQUET

On 24 October, thanks largely to the Duchess'
energy and influence, we received a telegram
from British Head-Quarters ordering us to start
for Boulogne in twenty-four hours. The same
evening the Duchess, the Matron (an old acquaintance of mine) and one of the Medical
Officers returned from Boulogne with the news
that no building could be found for us there. Two
days later, however, we had orders to proceed to
Étaples, for which we left the next morning. Our
hospital 'kit' filled a dozen railway trucks; we
had sixty orderlies (a Bristol unit of the St John
Ambulance Association), nineteen Bart.'s nurses
and four unqualified dressers. Our commandant
was Major H. E. M. Douglas, R.A.M.C., V.C.,
D.S.O., who had already a gallant record in the
regular army; the senior surgeon was Major (now

Sir) Charles Gordon Watson, F.R.C.S., on the staff of St Bartholomew's Hospital; and the rest of the surgical and medical staff included five Medical Officers (all with temporary commissions), a quartermaster (with honorary commission), a friend of the latter and myself (without commissions).

We left Paris at 1.40 p.m. from the Gare S. Chapelle, a goods station near the Gare du Nord. Our orderlies arrived decked with flowers presented to them on their march to the station. The greetings of the men and the kisses of the women of Paris were unrestrained. It was everywhere, 'les braves Anglais'. As soon as I had donned khaki, little girls came up begging me for a souvenir; young women bade me 'good morning'; boys sang 'God save the King'; and old ladies stopped me to argue about the Kaiser's then recent phrase, "that contemptible little army". But Paris was in a sorry plight, and we were glad enough to leave it for the work we had come out to do. In our walks in the Bois, we noticed that most of the people were dressed in black. Several of the roads were barred: no traffic was allowed, for instance, through the Porte Maillot, the road beyond being interrupted by deep trenches and protected by huge logs of wood. Quantities of cattle were herded just outside the city gates in a grassless enclosure, and were being fed from stacks of hay. The Paris hospitals were being emptied of army patients as rapidly as possible. Still, the rather trying time of delay in Paris passed without undue boredom, occupied in visits to the military and civil hospitals, colleagues and friends, chief among which I recall those I paid to Professors Bergson, Boutroux and Déjerine.

We reached Étaples at 10.30 p.m., proceeding by Épluches and Belmont, as the Chantilly route was interrupted owing to the blowing up of the bridges across the Oise. At Creil we passed houses burnt by the petrol squirts of the Germans. At Étaples we proceeded by tramway to the Casino at Le Touquet, which the Duchess had secured for her hospital. We were lodged at the Hôtel des Anglais, close by.

The three following days were spent in unpacking the instruments, dressings, tables, linen, crockery, etc., which the unit had brought out from England. We made our first acquaintance with the plage at Le Touquet, the sand dunes, the woods and the well-known golf links. Of the golf club, we were informed, we were to be made honorary members; but none of us attempted to play before having really got into harness. The flags were still flying and a ground-man was rolling the greens; but such care soon became a thing of the past.

Boulogne was at that time crowded with British wounded. Funerals were passing all day.

Men were lying about the station, waiting to be taken to England. Meanwhile Le Touquet, close to Étaples on the main line from Boulogne to Paris, waited several days in vain for patients. I heard that (the late) Sir Arthur Sloggett, Director-General of the Medical Services of the British Forces in the Field, who had recently come out from England, had promised to do his best for us and to visit our hospital, but he had been given the wrong impression that Étaples lay in a *cul-de-sac* and was very 'ungetatable'.

On 4 November Major Douglas, our Commandant, went into Boulogne and returned with the promise of a hospital train that day. At about 7.45 p.m. the first cases arrived from Étaples station by ambulance car. The men had been travelling from St Omer since 11 a.m.; they looked worn out, and the more serious wounds badly needed re-dressing. The procession of cars, going and returning, continued until 1 a.m., and we did not get to bed until after 2 a.m.

The next day we were up at 8 a.m., dressing the wounded soon after 9 a.m. I had been appointed Registrar and Assistant Physician, and my first duties consisted in preparing lists of the 200 patients, with their names, ranks, regimental numbers, regiments, etc. With no one to help me, I was occupied until 2.15 a.m. the next morning in this work. Fresh cases arrived that day. I shared an office with the Commandant, whom I helped with his correspondence. I started two card-indexes of the patients admitted, one according to their names, the other according to the injury or disease from which they were suffering. This seemed to be the first effort of its kind in the Army Medical Service, if I may judge from the interest which the Director-General and other high officers of the Army Medical Service showed in it. When they paid their first visit to the hospital, they were brought round to my 'registrary' and shown the advantages of the method. I had sent for the cards from England, finding the system of classification in the official Hospitals Admission and Discharge Books of the British Army very imperfect, both as it stood and in its relation to conditions of present warfare. All our visitors expressed their delight with our hospital. The spacious entrance hall led on the right to a large medical ward, and on the left to a larger surgical ward; beyond lay a still larger room (used in peace time for the Casino gaming tables) which served as a second surgical ward. Upstairs, approached through a gallery running round the hall, were the offices, the operating theatre and instrument room and an Officers' ward. A pathological laboratory and an X-ray room were installed on the ground floor. We had at that time 260 beds, but later the whole hospital was used for Officers only, and the number of beds was materially reduced.

Many of our cases in those early days came direct from the Front, having been on the train, in one instance, for thirty-six hours. The stories they told were often of a ghastly nature. One man informed me that he had seen a German shoot a wounded British Officer. Another described to me how the Germans had overrun his trench and killed the sixteen wounded who were left there, firing on some, bayonetting others. He himself lay with his head under a fallen body shamming death, and a German Officer listened to see if he breathed, finally passing him by putting a bullet into his leg. He heard his comrades shrieking "Murder". Other stories were of a better order. A gunner, for example, told me of a British Officer who was slightly wounded by the Germans on emerging from his trench in an attempt to rescue a wounded German Officer. The Germans at once ceased firing and allowed the British Officer to stagger beneath his burden to the German lines. Thereupon a German Officer presented him with his iron cross, and the firing was not resumed until the British Officer had had ample time to return to his trench.

My time at the Duchess of Westminster's Hospital was at first fully occupied in registrar's work, but the Commandant had promised me some beds as soon as I had more leisure. I began to train orderlies to help me in my routine duties, and thoroughly enjoyed my work. We were a very happy family, and it was only when at length I was given charge of some cases that difficulties arose and I began to realize the differences between an academic and a medical career. Several of the Medical Officers on our staff were young consultants in civil life. Now the life of a rising Harley Street specialist is one of ceaseless push and of considerable anxiety. He is continually on the look-out for the crumbs of practice dropped by his senior colleagues. He takes an expensive house or consulting rooms far beyond his means, and invests in a large motor car, speculating on his future success. No wonder is it, then, that self-seeking and jealousy enter so much more into his life than into one previously spent, like mine, in the quieter backwaters of a University town. To this I attribute the situation which temporarily developed when, in view of the great amount of clinical material, Majors Douglas and Watson made over some medical cases to me. After a few days' trial I saw that it was advisable to ask to be relieved of them, and I gave myself up to the duller routine of a registrar's work.

The Duchess had worked with wonderful energy for the opening of her unit. Later I heard from the War Office official who had consented to its starting from England that he had got into trouble for giving this permission. Not unnaturally, the Medical Service in France was, at first at all events, opposed to such independent units. After overcoming this opposition, the Duchess did excellent work each day in the linen room. Various of her friends in 'high society' came to visit the magnificent hospital, at that time the finest in France. The treatment and the nursing of the patients were all that could be desired. But discipline, in the strict military sense, was not to be expected; there were apt to be, in the words of the Commandant, "too many captains in the ship". And so the inevitable mixture of civil and army *régime* proved too much for him. On 20 November, to my great regret, Major Douglas ceased to be Commandant of the unit, and was transferred to duty elsewhere in France; Major Gordon Watson succeeded him.

On 9 December the Director-General, Sir Arthur Sloggett, when visiting the hospital, offered me a temporary commission as Captain in the R.A.M.C. The idea seemed humorous to him: "We'll make a dashin' Captain of you", he remarked in his usual jaunty way.

In December I had the opportunity of carrying out some investigations on the sensibility of the feet of soldiers suffering from what later came to be known as 'trench foot'. I collated also the notes of over 150 cases in the hospital. They were published together in the *British Medical Journal.*

During the previous month I saw for the first time one of those cases of 'functional' mental and nervous disorder, which afterwards proved so plentiful and came to receive the name of 'shell shock'. This patient was a man near whom several shells had burst, in his endeavour to disentangle himself from barbed wire during retirement over open ground. Immediately after one of the shells had burst in front of him, his sight, he said, became blurred. Another shell which then burst behind him gave him a greater shock—"like a punch on the head, without any pain after it". The shell in front cut his haversack clean away and bruised his side, and apparently it burned his fingers. This man was found to be suffering from 'functionally' contracted fields of vision, loss of smell and taste, and slight impairment of visual acuity. Two other cases, respectively due to a shell blowing in a trench, and blowing the patient off a wall, were characterized by similar 'functional' symptoms and by well-marked loss of memory. The second of these three cases was the first in which I attempted successfully to restore the patient's memory by means of slight hypnosis. I published these cases in the *Lancet* of 13 February 1915; and in a second communication to the same journal, issued on 8 January 1916, I emphasized the undoubted therapeutic value of the early restoration of lost memories in such cases.

In the former of these papers I must have been one of the first to use the term 'shell shock', which has since deservedly received adverse criticism. But I was careful to point out the "close relations of these cases to those of 'hysteria'"; and I did not suppose, as Lieut.-Col. (the late Sir) Frederick Mott was then attempting to show, that they arose from the effects of minute cerebral haemorrhages or other microscopically visible lesions. I attributed them, as they are now generally attributed, to mental 'repression' and 'dissociation', but I was inclined to lay some emphasis on the physical shock produced by the bursting of a shell as a prime cause of the 'dissociation'. Later familiarity with the disorder, however, showed that emotional disturbance alone was a sufficient cause, and thus led to the neglect of possible factors of a physical nature. This I believed to be an error. I was at first by no means convinced that all cases of 'functional dissociation' arose *solely* from mental causes. The high-frequency vibrations caused by an exploding shell might, it seemed to me, conceivably produce an invisibly fine 'molecular' commotion in the brain which, in turn, might produce dissociation, either "through its exhaustive effect on the higher 'intellectual' regions or through its excessive stimulant effect on the lower 'emotional' regions", as I remarked in a later article in the *Lancet* of 11 January 1919. Since all the early cases that came under my notice followed from the shock (whether mental or physical) of an exploding shell, the choice of the term 'shell shock' did not seem inappropriate, although in the sequel, as I shall point out, it proved unsatisfactory.

DEPARTURE FROM LE TOUQUET

On 30 January 1915 I had a conversation with the neurological specialist, Lieut.-Col. Aldren Turner, a Territorial Officer in the R.A.M.C., who had been sent out by the War Office from England as its Consultant Neurologist, to report on the now increasing number of cases of 'shell shock' and on "the conditions under which their treatment should be carried out to the best advantage both during the preliminary stages in France and afterwards on their arrival" in England. By this time it was clear to me that my previous psychological training and my present interests fitted me for the treatment of these cases. I also met the now distinguished neurologist, Lieut.-Col. (then Major) Gordon Holmes, who was working at Boulogne with the skilful 'brain surgeon', the late Col. (then Lieut.-Col.) Percy Sargent, on the war lesions of the nervous system; and he spontaneously exclaimed—"How I wish you could join us by undertaking the psychological work in this district!" With this object Lieut.-Col. Sargent gave me a letter to take with me to General Sir Alfred Keogh, Director-General of the Army Medical Service, at the War Office, whom I saw during my first leave (1–5 February).

Shortly after my return to France I heard that Lieut.-Col. Turner was taking steps for me to replace him in the duties which he had come over to France to perform; and on 20 and 25 February he visited me to discuss the details of this work, and to obtain from me my exact qualifications which he could transmit in a letter to Sir Alfred Keogh. On 16 March, not without some regret, I handed over my registrar's work to my successor and left the Duchess of Westminster's Hospital for Boulogne, in order to spend a few days with Col. Turner before his return to England. On 25 March I received a copy of a letter from Sir Alfred Keogh to Sir Arthur Sloggett, dated 19 March, informing him that "the appointment of Temporary Captain C. S. Myers to succeed Lieut.-Colonel W. A. Turner in his special duties is approved. He will be granted the temporary rank, pay and allowance of Major. The date he assumes duty should be reported." On 28 March I was attached to the staff of the Assistant (later Deputy) Director of Medical Services, Boulogne, and on 6 April I reported at General Head-Quarters, St Omer, on assuming my new duties.

THE GROWTH OF MY NEW WORK

Those of Lieut.-Col. Turner's duties which I took over on 28 March 1915 were officially described as follows: "to select suitable cases of nervous and mental shock and neurasthenia for transference to the appropriate institutions in England for treatment". But in the course of time they became much more numerous and far-reaching. They were gradually extended (a) to advising on and visiting wards provided for all cases of mental disorder and disease, including cases of insanity; (b) to supervising and assisting in the treatment of such cases; (c) to advising in cases of suspected malingering; (d) to examining, and giving Court-martial evidence on, soldiers charged with desertion, suicide, drunkenness, or other crimes; (e) to sitting on numerous Medical Boards; (f) to examining and diagnosing purely neurological cases (organic lesions in the brain and spinal cord); (g) to differentiating cases of 'functional' from those of 'organic' disorder, etc. I vainly pointed out that no expert could be found who would claim special knowledge in all of these kinds of work. For my part, I had had no special 'Asylum' experience, nor had I a specialist's knowledge of neurological diseases. But an Army Medical Officer has to obey commands. They arose in my case partly from ignorance on the part of those who issued them, and partly from the fact that at the time when I began to work on cases of insanity there was no one else available in France. In the Royal Army Medical Corps there were Officers with special knowledge of surgery, pathology, etc., some of whom had achieved a world-wide reputation;

but I never met with a regular Officer who had had any specialist's training and experience in mental or nervous diseases and disorders.

AT BOULOGNE

I remained at Boulogne until the middle of January 1916, except for six weeks which I spent in Casualty Clearing Stations close to the Front, at Bailleul, Poperinghe and Béthune, where I had the opportunity of studying 'shell shock' in its earliest stages, occasionally visiting Field Ambulances and Advanced Dressing Stations. While at Boulogne, I visited every day the various General and Stationary Hospitals there and at Wimereux and Étaples, where 'shell shock' cases were admitted; I examined and advised upon all the so-called 'mental' and '? mental' cases at Boulogne Base, selecting suitable cases for transference to D Block of the Royal Victoria Hospital, Netley, or to the neurological section of that Hospital, or of the 4th London General Hospital, besides serving as a member of all the Medical Boards appointed at that Base to report on soldiers charged with some offence and admitted for observation as to their sanity and responsibility.

AT ST OMER

From the middle of January 1916, when I received the rank of Lieutenant-Colonel, I was stationed at General Head-Quarters (St Omer), through which all 'mental' and '? mental' cases were passing from the First Army and some from the Second Army. Nearly one-third of those whom I saw I returned to duty, with only one known case of relapse. Of the remainder, some were sent to the Mental Ward at Boulogne, some to ordinary wards at St Omer or Boulogne, and others to 'rest'. From St Omer I continued to visit the Base hospitals as before, including also Le Tréport, Rouen, and Dieppe; I also saw many cases at various Casualty Clearing Stations in the Front Areas.

AT ABBEVILLE

On the removal of General Head-Quarters from St Omer, towards the end of May 1916, I became attached to the Director of Medical Services, Lines of Communication, at Abbeville, whence I visited the Mental Wards at the various Bases, which were increasing in number, planning the construction (or re-construction) of these wards, and advising on certain mental and 'shell shock' cases, etc., in Front Areas and at the Bases as heretofore.

DIVISION OF DUTIES

In the middle of August 1916 the title previously given me of "Specialist in Nerve Shock" was changed to "Consulting Psychologist". By the end of that year expert mental specialists had been

appointed to the various Bases provided with
Mental Wards, and 80 per cent. of my visits were
being paid to Front Areas. Receiving 'centres'
were now, at length, being appointed at the rear
of the latter, which treated the readily curable
cases of 'shell shock', most of those evacuated to
the Bases being henceforth sent to England. In
these altered circumstances I was about to suggest
to the Director of Medical Services, Lines of
Communication, that my headquarters should be
moved nearer to the Front, when, to my surprise,
he announced to me a new arrangement that I
should have control of 'shell shock', 'mental' and
'neurological' cases occurring within the Fourth
and Fifth Army Areas and at Dieppe, Le Tréport,
Rouen and Havre, leaving the remaining Areas
and Bases to Lieut.-Col. Gordon Holmes who,
having recently relinquished his neurological
partnership with the surgeon, Col. Percy Sargent,
was seeking other specialist work. Col. Holmes
had previously asked me whether, under the
altered conditions of his work, I had any objection
to his undertaking the treatment of 'functional'
cases at the Base; but I did not foresee that my
immediate consent would entail such a radical
change and restriction in my work.

The proper course would have been for him to
be employed in diagnosing and advising on the
treatment of strictly neurological cases throughout all hospitals and for me to continue my 'shell

shock' and 'mental' work as before, each calling in the other in doubtful cases, when the use of his special experience was desirable. But Col. Holmes informed me that he had been also induced to approach General Head-Quarters because, having been appointed Consulting Neurologist at the same time as I was appointed Consulting Psychologist, he felt himself responsible for the 'shell shock' cases, although, he confessed, he felt quite incompetent to examine 'mental' cases.

Thus it came about that the Director-General bisected the King Solomon's baby claimed by two 'mothers'! Col. Holmes had previously told me that functional 'nervous' disorders always formed a very large part of the civilian neurologist's practice. Naturally, therefore, he was little disposed to relinquish in Army life what was so important a source of income in time of peace, although he confessed that (like most 'pure' neurologists) he took little interest in such cases. During the past twenty-five years, however, thanks to the work of Janet, Prince, Freud, Jung, Adler, Hart, Rows, Jones and many others, the position has now changed: the neurologist's methods of treating the psycho-neuroses have been very largely superseded by those of the psycho-therapist. These are fundamentally opposed, the former, usually ignorant of normal and abnormal psychology, being content to treat patent symptoms and signs by persuasion or force, the latter aiming primarily at the discovery and abolition of their underlying conscious and unconscious mental origins and maintaining that it is useless to deal with the results and to neglect their causes, if a permanent cure is to be expected.

I addressed a private letter to the Director-General of Medical Services, calling his attention to the fact that the recent rearrangement of my duties had resulted in my being called upon to undertake work (viz. the diagnosis of lesions and organic diseases of the brain and cord) which I felt unqualified to perform. But no action was taken. By January 1917 I had become so worn out with worry over the conditions of my work that I put in a request for prolonged leave in England, or alternatively I offered the Director-General of Medical Services my resignation. I was granted two months' sick leave, on my return from which to France I resumed my work under the old conditions.

VISIT TO FRENCH ARMY HOSPITALS

In June 1917 I asked if arrangements could be made for me to visit certain of the so-called 'neurological' and 'neuro-psychiatric' centres attached to the French Armies and to certain areas in the French 'intérieur'. Through the kind offices of the Adjutant-General and the Director-General of Medical Services, permission was obtained for me to visit the 'Neurological Centre' of the 6th *Région* at Châlons-sur-Marne; and at Paris, in the following month, I was able to arrange for visits to be paid by me also to other 'centres' at Château-Thierry, Besançon, Salins, Lyons and Tours. I was away for two weeks and on my return prepared, at the request of the Director-General of Medical Services, a statement embodying the special features which I had observed during my visit (see pp. 102–107).

CONFERENCE IN LONDON

In October 1917 I attended a Conference in London presided over by Sir Alfred Keogh, Director-General of Medical Services at the War Office, who asked me to remain in London to attend the subsequent meetings of a Committee appointed at this Conference to draw up a scheme of treatment and administration in regard to the 'shell shock' cases in hospitals in Great Britain. After a week of daily meetings and the preparation of a report, the Committee adjourned to meet again in a week's time, and I returned to France.

DEPARTURE FROM FRANCE

I was so much impressed with what I could do to improve conditions in Great Britain in the light of my two and a half years' experience in France, and I felt so strongly that I had done all that I was likely to be able to do in France, that I wrote to

Sir Arthur Sloggett, with the confidential approval (and indeed encouragement) of Sir Alfred
Keogh, informing him of my wish to return to
England at the end of the year. My desire to be
relieved of duties overseas was not opposed; and
in November I received instructions from the
War Office, through General Head-Quarters, to
return to England. On my arrival Sir Alfred
Keogh informed me that he hoped to make use
of me at the War Office. He had previously sent
me a letter to this effect, saying "how gladly I
should welcome you amongst us here, not merely
because of your knowledge of your subject, but
because your matured experience of Army affairs
will help to regulate the wilder spirits who lack a
due sense of proportion".

Chapter II

THE FEATURES AND CAUSATION OF 'SHELL SHOCK'

BY the middle of 1916 Col. Turner was able, after a further visit to France, to report that satisfactory arrangements had now been made by me whereby cases of 'neurasthenia' and 'nervous breakdown' were specially labelled on their departure from the Base hospitals by Medical Officers with proper qualifications for this work.

By that time I had myself seen upwards of two thousand cases of 'shell shock', in addition to numerous cases of other mental disorder, and I had treated a considerable proportion of these. At the request of various Medical Officers at the Front, I had begun to put together the results of my experience of 'shell shock' and towards the end of the year I requested permission to publish (virtually) the contents of this and the next chapter of this book, suggesting that they would prove acceptable in the various hospitals in Army Areas and also in Great Britain where cases of 'shell shock' were, or would be, received for treatment. I was informed, however, by the Director-General of Medical Services that as the

General Staff was at the moment strongly opposed to the publication of articles on 'shell shock', the best use that could be made of the paper would be to communicate it confidentially to the medical units in Army Areas that were, or would be, receiving cases of 'shell shock'.

DEFINITION AND SYMPTOMS OF 'SHELL SHOCK'

After a man has been buried, lifted or otherwise subjected to the physical effects of a bursting shell or other similar explosive, he may suffer solely from concussion (which should be termed 'shell concussion'), or solely from mental 'shock' (so-called 'shell shock'), or from both of these conditions in succession.

If 'shell shock' occurs, it will give rise to one or more of the following groups of mental symptoms, namely, (i) hysteria, (ii) neurasthenia, (iii) graver temporary 'mental' disorder.

But 'shell shock' and these three groups of accompanying symptoms (which will receive closer examination presently) do not depend for their causation on the physical force (or the chemical effects) of the bursting shell. They may also occur when the soldier is remote from the exploding missile, provided that he be subject to an emotional disturbance or mental strain sufficiently severe. Apart from the effects of complicating concussion (or, in its milder form, 'commotion'), there are no mental signs in 'shell shock' pathognomonic of the *physical* effects of an exploding shell on the central nervous system, which enable us to distinguish them from the *psychical* effects following on a purely mental disturbance, where the tolerable or controllable limits of horror, fear, anxiety, etc., are over-stepped.

A shell, then, may play no part whatever in the causation of 'shell shock': excessive emotion, e.g. sudden horror or fear—indeed any 'psychical trauma' or 'inadjustable experience'—is sufficient. Moreover, in men already worn out or having previously suffered from the disorder, the final cause of the breakdown may be so slight, and its onset so gradual, that its origin hardly deserves the name of 'shock'. 'Shell shock', therefore, is a singularly ill-chosen term; and in other respects, as we shall see, it has proved a singularly harmful one.

Shell concussion. Of this little need be said beyond a passing reference to the difficulties which may sometimes arise (*a*) in distinguishing the severest cases of stupor from cases of severe concussion and (*b*) in distinguishing the latter from cases of other organic lesion. Of course, signs of bruising of the head, a feeble, easily com-pressible pulse and cold clammy extremities favour a diagnosis of concussion and contra-indicate stupor. There may be special difficulty

in those cases of spinal concussion (perhaps complicated by trivial haemorrhage), which simulate
organic spinal injuries and which recover despite
initial incontinence of the bladder and rectum
and other apparently grave signs. In certain cases
of 'shell shock' increased pressure of, and other
changes (e.g. the presence of albumin and leuco-
cytosis) in, the cerebro-spinal fluid have been
observed; these, however, are usually a result of
the concussion (or 'commotion') simultaneously
sustained, although they may be sometimes due
merely to the 'psychical trauma' incurred.

Neurasthenic sequelae. Strictly speaking, neurasthenia (with which certain features of 'psy-
chasthenia' may be here included) is a mental and
nervous disorder due to exhaustion. Its chief
symptoms, as observed in cases of 'shell shock',
are abnormal irritability, depression, loss of confidence, loss of power of concentration, headache,
giddiness, asthenopia, general fatigability and
loss of sleep and appetite. It may also give rise
to obsessions, anxieties, fears, and delusions
(especially of persecution). Clinically it is sometimes difficult to draw a sharp line between the
symptoms of this group and those of the two
other groups which they may complicate and
facilitate, although usually, and in origin, their
natures are very different.

Hysteric sequelae. While the neurasthenic
worries consciously over his troubles, in the

hysteric they are commonly relegated to the unconscious. The neurasthenic remains an intact,
though worn out, individual, whereas (more or
less recognizably) the personality of the hysteric
has changed. The breakdown in the neurasthenic
is due to persistent wear and tear; in the hysteric
(and in the 'mental' group of sequelae) this is
avoided by a sudden snap or fission, whereby
certain nervous or mental processes are 'functionally dissociated', or 'unconsciously repressed'
by inhibition, from the rest. Neurasthenia may
be regarded as a common accident, hysteria as a
necessary result of severe 'shell shock'.

The resulting manifestations of such 'functional dissociation' in the hysteric group may be
classified as (*a*) inhibitory, (*b*) excitatory, and
(*c*) ataxic, according to the nature of the partial or
complete loss of control by the individual over
sensory, perceptual, or motor functions or (often
indirectly) by the lower reflex centres over their
unconsciously co-ordinated mechanisms. These
manifestations may be conveniently tabulated
according to the annexed scheme (p. 30), which,
however, makes no pretence to completeness,
nor indeed wholly to physiological accuracy.

In general, as might be expected, tremor,
sweating, and a rapid pulse are more frequently
associated with excitement or horror than with
cowed or depressed states. Stammering is, more
frequently than aphasia, accompanied by in-

coordination of other movements, pseudo-Rombergism and pseudo-clonus, disturbance of sensibility and feebleness of gait. Extra-active (or feeble) flexor reflexes tend to go with extra-active (or feeble) responses of the pupil to light. Muscular rigidity, spasm and over-reaction, local aching and tenderness are commonly associated with hyperaesthesia; paresis, palsy, muscular tremor and local numbness with anaesthesia.[1]

'*Mental*' *sequelae*. The temporary 'mental' disorders resulting from 'shell shock' are likewise due mainly to 'dissociation'. They include transient, uncontrollable excitement and other recurring emotional outbursts, confusional and stuporose states, hallucinations, delusions, obsessions, anxieties, fugues and such other changes in personality as alternations of personality, amnesia, extreme suggestibility, etc. They are causally related in part to the neurasthenic, and in part to the hysteric, group of symptoms which I have distinguished.

CAUSATION

Post-mortem examination. Several fatal cases of so-called 'shell shock' (which should have been distinguished as 'shell concussion') have been examined *post-mortem*, where death has occurred

[1] A full account of my observations in France on disorders of cutaneous sensibility in 'shell shock' will be found in my article in the *Lancet* of 18 March 1916.

	Inhibitory	Excitatory	Ataxic
(a) *Conscious* Sensory level	'Functional' loss of sight, hearing, smell, etc., restriction of visual fields, anaesthesia, superficial or deep analgesia, etc.	'Functional' over-reaction to visual, auditory, tactual, etc., stimuli. Hyperaesthesia, hyperalgesia, etc.	—
Perceptual level	'Functional' loss of awareness of meaning in regard to objects seen, grasped, etc., or of sounds heard; the sensibility to light, touch, sound, etc., being nevertheless retained	—	—
Simple movement	'Functional' paresis or palsy of voluntary muscles, e.g., aphonia, mono-, hemi- or para-plegia, etc.	'Functional' spasmodic or convulsive movements, contractures, etc.	'Functional' ataxia of simple movements
Complex movement	'Functional' inability to perform skilled acts, e.g. in regard to speech, writing, walking, etc., although the power of uttering sounds, of moving the limbs, etc., is retained	'Functional' obsessive, symbolic and other persistent acquired actions	'Functional' dys-arthria (stammer), dys-basia, and other forms of dys-synergia
(b) *Automomic*	(?) 'Functional' muscular hypotonus, hypothermia, slowness of contraction, vascular dilatation, lowered blood-pressure, bradycardia, diminished reflexes, visceral disturbances, atrophic changes, etc.	(?) 'Functional' hypertonus and hyper-excitability of muscles, catatonia, spasticity, *pseudo-clonus, hyperidrosis, increased reflexes, dilatation of pupils, increased blood-pressure, tachycardia, pallor, visceral disturbances, etc.	'Functional' incoordination of other bodily and of visceral movements (*pseudo-ataxia, *pseudo-Rombergism, *pseudo-nystagmus, tremor, etc.) * See Note, p. 31.

within two or three days after a shell explosion had buried the patient, in whom no lesion to skin or bone could be detected. In one case, where consciousness was not lost until just before death, the spinal cord showed (among other changes) numerous small haemorrhages throughout the grey and white matter of the lower cervical region; this patient had been buried in a dug-out, and before death had shown complete paralysis of the limbs and of the intercostal muscles. In other cases of burial, of which most, if not all, were moribund on admission to hospital, the brain showed numerous petechial haemorrhages in the cerebral cortex and especially in the corpus callosum and basal ganglia, coalescing in places, particularly in the corpus callosum, into large areas of haemorrhage with widely destructive effects. The viscera may also be lacerated; even

---

* 'Pseudo' is prefixed because the phenomena are usually different from those observed in 'organic' nervous disease. Thus the clonus is usually of brief duration, disappearing when the degree of tension is changed; the ataxia is often hardly different whether the eyes are closed or open; the Rombergism commonly disappears when the patient's attention is distracted; the nystagmus is rather of the nature of an extreme unsteadiness. But exceptions to this rule occur: the same holds for changes in the reflexes, which are usually distinguishable from those in 'organic' cases. Some of these manifestations arise from immediate action on the sympathetic or cranio-spinal divisions of the autonomic nervous system, sometimes doubtless through the effects of the shock on the internal secretions, combined with local nervous predisposition, congenital or acquired. Others are of late origin and are apparently due to organic changes in the central or peripheral nervous system set up by long-continued 'functional' muscular disorders.

cases which ultimately recover may suffer immediately after burial from haemorrhage from the lungs, stomach, etc. So far as I am aware, no case of death from 'shell shock', occurring a week or longer after the incidence of the shock, has been recorded.

Relation to poisoning by carbon monoxide. A large amount of carbon monoxide is emitted by an exploding shell, and the suggestion has been advanced that the physical and mental results of 'shell shock' are due to the poisonous effects of this gas. In civil life the results attributed to carbonic-oxide poisoning happen to be so extraordinarily varied that there are few symptoms of 'shell shock' which cannot be found recorded in some case of carbonic-oxide poisoning. Hysteric contracture, clonic spasms, convulsions, paralysis, anaesthesia, hyperaesthesia, vertigo, incoordination, amnesia (even involving loss of memory of how to speak or to walk, and loss of the meaning of objects seen or of words heard), have all been described among the effects or sequelae of carbonic-oxide poisoning. Moreover, the *post-mortem* changes observed in fatal cases of poisoning by this gas in coal mines, etc., include punctiform haemorrhages in the cerebral cortex, in the corpus callosum and in the basal ganglia. Further, in cases of rapidly fatal poisoning, men have been found in the same attitude in which they were at the moment of the gas explosion, with food or implements in their hands—as indeed they undoubtedly have been found, presumably after shell explosions, during the present war; although on these latter, so far as I am aware, no necropsy has been performed.

But the adoption of the hypothesis that the symptoms of 'shell shock' are due to the action of carbon monoxide presents numerous difficulties, e.g.

(i) In no case of 'shell shock', so far as I am aware, has the presence of carbon monoxide been demonstrated in the blood of the patient. It has, however, been stated that carbon monoxide may kill before it has had time to enter into combination with the haemoglobin. On the other hand, under war conditions, carbon monoxide is unlikely to be present in such concentration as to cause death or severe symptoms except when the soldier is exposed to it underground.

(ii) Among the effects or sequelae of carbon monoxide poisoning there have been described pneumonia, Cheyne-Stokes breathing, epistaxis, hiccough, cherry-coloured erythematous patches on the skin, neuritis and oedema (especially in paralytic cases). But none of these has been observed in cases of 'shell shock'.

(iii) When carbon monoxide is present in smaller quantities, its effects include ringing in the ears, lassitude, loss of power in limbs, throbbing or fluttering of the heart, and a rise of temperature on recovery. None of these symptoms can be regarded as *characteristic* of 'shell shock'.

(iv) The deaths following exposure to *ordinary* shell gases (excluding, that is to say, those obviously due to expressly devised *toxic* gases) have all occurred within a few days after the explosion. But in fatal cases of carbon-monoxide poisoning, sudden death has been recorded in patients who were believed to have recovered from its effects, and relapses are common after the patient has been improving for a considerable time.

In the face of these difficulties, it is probably truer to say that many of the symptoms formerly attributed to carbon monoxide are due to the mental shock received at the moment of the explosion than that the symptoms of 'shell shock' are due to carbon-monoxide poisoning.

Relation to changes in atmospheric pressure. There can be no doubt that the changes in atmospheric pressure produced in the neighbourhood of an exploding shell are enormous, and that they are capable of causing profound cerebral or spinal commotion or even sudden death, with or without haemorrhages in the central nervous system. It is, of course, possible that haemorrhages have occurred also in the case of some of those who continue to live after being exposed to such conditions. But we have no conclusive evidence that the haemorrhages or the physical commotion induced by the abrupt and severe changes of pressure are the direct cause of the signs of 'shell shock', although such a physical causation is not inconceivable.

From the foregoing all that we seem entitled to conclude is that abrupt changes in atmospheric pressure, or exposure to carbon-monoxide gas or physical violence, resulting from the explosion of a shell, may each produce haemorrhages and other minute lesions within the central nervous system, and that such disorganization may favour, although it is not essential for, the development of the symptoms observed in 'shell shock'.

Relation to internal secretions. It is well recognized that the signs and symptoms of hyperthyroidism, or even of definite Graves' disease, may occur after great fear, worry or rage. It has also been established that emotional excitement of any kind leads to excessive adrenal activity, causing an increase in the amount of adrenalin, hence of sugar, in the blood, and even producing temporary glycosuria. It is, therefore, conceivable that some of the symptoms of 'shell shock', e.g. changes in the blood pressure, pulse rate, sweating, nervousness, etc., which may occur, are due to increased glandular secretion of this nature. But neither the clinical observations I have made on blood pressure and urine, nor the administration of glandular extracts, in early cases of 'shell shock', has established, in my experience, a definite and necessary connexion between 'shell shock' and disordered internal secretion. It is, however, to be borne in mind that the different symptoms of 'shell shock', instead of being due to the exhaustion or excessive activity of any single internally secreting gland, may conceivably arise from a varying complex simultaneous disorder of several glands, the result of a mixed autonomic neurosis.*

Relation to mental condition. In the vast majority of cases the signs of 'shell shock' (apart from those of 'shell concussion') appear traceable to psychical causes, especially, in the early cases, to the emotions of extreme and sudden horror or fright. Probably, however, they may also occur when the physical or mental shock has been so abrupt and so severe as to produce immediate loss of consciousness before the above emotions have been experienced in consciousness. Previous emotional disorder, worry, insomnia and, above all, a psycho-neurotic predisposition favour the onset of the shock and help to determine the nature of the mental and nervous sequelae.

* I recall two cases of 'shell shock' lying side by side in a Casualty Clearing Station, from both of which I elicited pronounced dermatographia. But in the one the 'writing' appeared in red (the well-known *tache cérébrale*), whereas in the other it appeared in white (the 'white line' of arterial hypotension often associated with disordered secretion of the adrenal and thyroid glands).

As has been already indicated, these sequelae may appear not only among those who have been buried or lifted by a shell, but also among others who have been bombed or mined, and in those who have never been near to any such exploding missile, or have not for some months been under shellfire, or indeed have never come under fire at all. They may assume, as we have seen, a preponderatingly neurasthenic, hysteric or 'mental' type; they may appear as disorders of emotion, intelligence, memory, sensation, perception, or voluntary movement, or even of certain mechanisms (e.g. of the circulation, of the motor reflexes, of the alimentary canal) which are not under the control of the will. Moreover, they have, for the most part, been previously recognized in civil life as occurring in industrial and railway accidents; to them the terms 'traumatic neurasthenia' and 'traumatic hysteria' have been applied. For yet another reason, then, the term 'shell shock' seems a needless innovation.

CONTRIBUTORY CONDITIONS

Recent strain. Long-continued fear, horror, anxiety, worry, previous 'shell shock', persistent 'sticking at it', exposure and fatigue are the most important factors under this head. There can be little doubt that insomnia, dyspepsia and constipation are also important predisposing factors. Adequate sleep is difficult to obtain in the trenches, and, even when 'in reserve', men may have to be employed in night-working parties; the regularity of the bowels, the state of the teeth and digestion are also prone to suffer in trench warfare.

Psycho-pathic predisposition. A large number of cases, especially of those who break down merely under the stress of warfare, occur in 'nervous' (psycho-neurotic) subjects who have previously suffered from mental conflicts and maladjustments, from 'fits' in childhood or from other 'nervous' attacks or breakdown. But even those who start with the strongest 'nerves' are not immune from 'shell shock', if exposed to sufficiently often repeated, or to incessant, strain, or if subjected to severe enough shock. Of 'nervous' subjects, however, two types must be recognized, the good and the bad: the former, often a highly intelligent person, keeping full control over his unduly sensitive nervous system; the latter, usually of feebler intellect, having little hold over his instinctive acts to escape danger, the emotions which impel him to them, and the resulting conflicts.

Discipline and self-control. If two units be exposed to the same conditions of shell fire at the same moment, the number of cases of 'shell shock' is found to be very appreciably greater in the less disciplined unit. The one will have been taught to take safe shelter individually; the other, with less self-control and *esprit de corps*, will herd together in insecure places, the shells falling on which may cause grave bodily injuries to some, and 'shell shock' to others from the effects upon them of these sights. There can be no doubt that, other things being equal, the frequency of 'shell shock' in any unit is an index of its lack of discipline and loyalty.

Much undoubtedly can be done, alike by combatant and medical Regimental Officers, to lessen the number of 'shell shock' cases by reducing the ill-effects of expectancy and want of control. But expectancy, it should be remembered, like the 'nervous' temperament, works both for good and for evil. A soldier who is well prepared for the effects of a coming shell may thus acquire better control over his emotions; on the other hand, of course, past experience will rouse alarm in the weakly, and a fatalistic conviction that the shell is 'meant' for him, during the interval between the hearing of the coming shell and its actual arrival.

When men have left the trenches and arrive tremulous or even mentally confused at the Aid Post, the Regimental Medical Officer who has won the confidence and respect of his unit may still combat their condition by the aid of moral suasion, and he may thereby successfully induce them to return to duty; whereas if once sent down to a Field Ambulance and thence farther down the Line, it may take many weeks or months before they are again fit for duty.

It is hardly surprising, then, that the very recognition of the term 'shell shock' as a disease is
liable to promote its frequency. Like all emotional
disorders, 'shell shock' is of a highly contagious
nature; it may be rife in one unit, while rare,
because regarded as a disgrace, in another.

The symptoms exhibited by Officers are predominantly of the neurasthenic type, whereas
those exhibited by the men are predominantly of
the hysteric type. As has been already pointed
out, the neurasthenic symptoms of the former are
due to a continuous 'wearing' emotion, or rather
mood; the hysteric symptoms of the latter are
due to a sudden 'breaking' emotion, or rather
'trauma'. The reasons for this difference are not
hard to find. The forces of education, tradition and
example make for greater self-control in the case
of the Officer. He, moreover, is busy throughout
a bombardment, issuing orders and subject to
worry over his responsibilities, whereas his men
can do nothing during the shelling, but watch and
wait until the order is received for an advance.

Malingering. 'Pure' malingering, in which a
man in absolutely good health purposely counter-
feits the symptoms of a mental or nervous disorder, is comparatively rare.* But many cases

* It is perhaps commonest in cases of amnesia and of aphonia.
The relation of malingering to these latter and to other functional
disorders of speech will be found in an article by me in the
Lancet of 9 September 1916.

arise from its combination with the effects of conscious or unconscious suggestion, or from a voluntary and avoidable surrender by the soldier of his control over his emotions; they are then largely of the nature of self-inflicted (mental) wounds, and are of course in great part preventible by discipline and *esprit de corps*. It also frequently happens that, consciously or semiconsciously, patients exaggerate their distress or artificially prolong their symptoms, in order to retard their return to duty at the Front. Moreover, a quite involuntary exaggeration of prolongation of the patient's symptoms often arises from anxiety, sometimes of known origin, e.g. through worry over the verdict of an impending Medical Board or over home affairs, or sometimes of a seemingly irrational character due to the unconscious influence of quite irrevocable past mental troubles.

It is not uncommon for a patient, after being cured of some functional impairment of speech or limb movement, to state that a few days before his recovery he had felt that he could have spoken or moved the affected limb, or that he would soon be able to do so. Such patients are apt, often wrongly, to worry over the belief that they have been malingering, whereas the possibilities of plural 'co-conscious' personality and the effects of gradual recovery from dissociation are almost incalculable. Sometimes, too, a confession of malingering may be obtained from the patient, especially under promise of secrecy, by his Medical Officer after successful treatment; but here suggestion may have had undue influence. Even long experience can only lead to a highly probable diagnosis of 'pure' malingering: absolute certainty can only be reached by detection *in flagrante delicto*.

SOME CLINICAL FEATURES

The following sketches of a few, sometimes composite, but 'typical', early cases seen by me in France may help to give some conception of the varied initial manifestations of severe 'shell shock' and (in the last case) of neurasthenia.

1. A large 'heavy explosive' shell fell on a dug-out, killing two of the occupants and blowing two other men to the far end of it. One of the latter was helped down to the Aid Post in a somewhat dazed condition, unsteady in his gait and complaining of headache. He was kept at the Aid Post to spend the night there, but was found a little later wandering into the open, taking off his clothes, and explaining that he was going to bed. After four days' rest and treatment in a Field Ambulance, he was able to return satisfactorily to duty. The other man, a sergeant, was brought into the Aid Post on a stretcher, unable to stand or to give any coherent statement. By the time he was admitted into a Casualty Clearing Station, his condition had become one of pro-

nounced stupor, which continued for more than a fortnight, accompanied at first by fever. Legs at first in a state of rigidity, later flaccid. Plantar responses at first *pseudo-extensor; other reflexes normal. At first, retention of urine and faeces, relieved by catheterization and strong purgatives. Gradually he began to take notice of his surroundings and on the seventeenth day after burial he suddenly sat up in bed and spoke for a few minutes, evidently with reference to some trench experiences—"They're at it again. D'you see that one, Jim?" etc., then relapsing into stupor. He virtually recovered his normal personality in England, but deafness and mutism remained until one day he had a hysteric, convulsive seizure, after which he shouted orders given in the trenches and thereupon regained his hearing and speech.

2. This man had been buried by a shell eight months before, and for the past six months had been employed on police duty in a large town. Of late he had been worrying over his sick wife, sleeping badly and dreaming often of the time when he was buried. He had been a total abstainer from alcohol for many years. During the past three months he had had difficulty in speaking, at first only when excited; speech never affected before. He also began to have attacks of trembling which became gradually worse. Finally he was admitted to hospital for general, uncon-

* The prefix 'pseudo' indicates that the response differs from a true 'Babinski' reaction.

trollable, irregular, muscular spasms. When he tried to speak, the masseter and temporal muscles underwent clonic contraction. He ate and swallowed well. Knee jerks much exaggerated. Pseudo-clonus of left ankle and knee. Tremor (especially in extension) and pseudo-ataxia of arms when trying to touch his nose with eyes shut, especially left side. Abdominal reflexes exaggerated. Generally diminished sensibility to touch and pain, especially left side. On left side, visual field and visual acuity and hearing much reduced, and smell and taste lost. Pulse soft and rapid. Face flushed, hands warm. He was isolated from the other patients. By the aid of suggestion, the recollection of various scenes connected with his burial was restored to him, many of which were previously irrevocable. Transient hysteric convulsions and considerable emotional excitement accompanied the revival of these memories; but with the return of the latter the spasms became less and less violent, the speech improved and the hemi-hypaesthesia disappeared almost completely. He was successfully induced to face the previously suppressed memories with confidence and self-control, and was sent to England to complete his recovery.

3. This man was found wandering along a road a few miles behind the Front. Nothing could be got out of him. On arrival at the Base, he showed extreme apathy and amnesia, ignorance of

his home life, parentage, soldiering, etc. He complained principally of headache. His complexion was of clay colour. Pulse feeble, hands warm. Pupils widely dilated and sluggish. No nystagmus. Fields normal. No knee jerk obtained. Conjunctival and corneal reflexes sluggish. Abdominal and palatal reflexes normal. Plantar response and ankle jerk less marked on right limb. Right hemi-hypalgesia. Under hypnosis, he was quickly induced to give his name, number, and regiment, and he explained that he had been heavily shelled for three days in the trenches, that his nerves had been thoroughly shaken and that he began to suffer from attacks of dizziness during which he wandered into parts of the trenches where he had no business to be. On returning from the trenches, he began to 'feel queer' and wandered all night until he found himself near a hut where he took refuge. On waking from hypnosis, he successfully retained all the memories just recovered, and revived others besides. In voice and in general demeanour he at once became an absolutely different individual; his complexion changed to a healthy hue, his pupils became smaller and active and his pulse much stronger, his hypalgesia disappeared, and the plantar responses became almost equal. Delighted with his recovery, he returned after three weeks' rest to duty at the Front where he continued in good health.

4. After being subject to heavy bombardment, during which a shell burst close to him, this man was brought into the Aid Post because he could not be restrained from rushing over the parapet with bombs in broad daylight. At the Aid Post he could not give his name or regiment, and was only induced to go down to the Field Ambulance by a ruse. In bed he developed complete mutism and an extremely restless condition, from time to time turning his eyes and head as if following an imaginary object, after which he would withdraw his head beneath the bed-clothes in abject terror. Later, when out of bed, he began to have hystero-epileptic seizures, during which he would undoubtedly have hurt himself unless restrained,* and following which he evidently visualized his terrifying experiences in the trenches. He called out during these attacks, but afterwards he had no recollection of them and his mutism persisted. Between the attacks he seemed otherwise quite normal. On transfer to England, he began to suffer from bad dreams, and his hands and feet became blue and often sweated. Under good treatment he gradually mended, suddenly regaining his speech in alarm at a bomb dropped close to his hospital from a Zeppelin.

5. A man who had seen his greatest friend killed beside him developed the following

---

* I have seen other such 'seizures', certainly not truly epileptic, in which the patients have hurt themselves.

symptoms. At first he struck several of his comrades, but later he assumed a semi-stuporose condition, in which he would stare curiously at such objects as shining buttons and play with them as a child. He became depressed, tearful, vacant, speechless and heedless of what was said to him. His pupils were of moderate size and active. The movements of his limbs were normal and free from rigidity. He took no notice of a pin-prick until it had been repeated several times, whereupon he gazed at the spot without attempting to withdraw from the pricking. Knee and arm jerks brisk. Well-marked jaw jerk. Plantar and abdominal reflexes not obtained. Two days later, he suddenly sat up and exclaimed: "Where am I?" Then he got out of bed and sat by the fire, speaking quite intelligently to the orderly, but with no memory of his military life. After a few minutes he relapsed into his former state. The next day he became very restless, and on being quieted and assured that he was in hospital, he gradually came to himself, but had completely lost all memory of what had occurred since he left the trenches. He had to be evacuated in this condition to England, where, it was considered, he made a complete recovery. But after his return to duty in England, he began to complain of shakiness, bad dreams, attacks of headache and dizziness, which, when severe, caused 'fainting attacks'. Finally, after another sudden shock he was re-admitted to hospital, suffering from complete 'functional' paraplegia.

6. An officer, subjected to recent heavy firing, sleeplessness and anxiety, and having experienced a previous 'nervous breakdown', was near a bursting shell, although he was not knocked over by it. He lost control of himself, alternately laughing and crying. He tried to 'pull himself together', but found that it was impossible to 'carry on'. He lost confidence and often forgot orders that he had given or received. He could not concentrate his attention for long. He became abnormally irritable, and began to suspect his brother officers of talking about him. Finally his colonel sent him down. On arrival at the Base, he was found to be very depressed, with loss of flesh, appetite and sleep, and with a complexion of clay colour. Tremulous tongue. Reflexes normal. No nystagmus. Well-marked hippus and pseudo-Rombergism. Pulse 72, regular. Tremulous hands, when outstretched. He made a slow recovery with repeated relapses, until he admitted that he was worried by certain dreams and inexplicable ideas which were ultimately traced to a long forgotten emotional experience. With explanation, encouragement, and suggestion, however, he began to improve and was ultimately able to resume administrative duties, which he can do well so long as he does not allow himself to worry.

Chapter III

THE TREATMENT AND PSYCHO-PATHOLOGY OF 'SHELL SHOCK'

TREATMENT

THE disposal of those cases which show signs of severe concussion, of severe neurasthenia, or of persistent mental derangement, in addition to the 'functional' results of 'shell shock', scarcely raises difficulty. Unless the concussion or mental derangement is transient, or unless the neurasthenic symptoms are slight, a considerable period of rest and treatment is essential, and the patient should be evacuated at once to the Base and, if necessary, thence to the wards of a 'special' hospital in Great Britain.

There is, however, far less unanimity of opinion in regard to the immediate treatment of the hysteric and cognate 'mental' disorders of 'shell shock', unaccompanied by serious concussion or neurasthenia or by obstinate mental derangement. Extremists in one direction would urge that such symptoms are so closely akin to malingering that they demand the adoption of the strictest disciplinary measures. Or, believing that the more attention is paid to such patients the worse they will become, they advocate at least a studied neglect of them. Extremists in the opposite direction would subject them to a prolonged course of psycho-analysis, or would tend indiscriminately to pamper them.

The truth, of course, lies within these extreme attitudes. Although *pure* malingering, unaccompanied by mental disturbance, is rare, nevertheless, in certain cases of 'shell shock', and at certain stages of recovery, disciplinary action is of the greatest value, whereas in others the use of harshness or the suspicion that the patient is considered a malingerer serves only to intensify his symptoms or to provoke fresh ones. Each case must be treated on its own merits. In some, recovery can be induced by the policy of making light of the patient's condition. But the indiscriminate adoption of a policy of neglect is comparable to the dangerous inference that because certain cases, say of appendicitis, recover without surgical interference, no cases should therefore be submitted to operation. Indeed, there can be little doubt that, if left to themselves, the majority of 'shell shock' cases gradually become worse (or at least their recovery is retarded), owing to the fixation of their attention on their present condition and on their past experiences.

The successful immediate treatment of such cases of 'shell shock' essentially consists in

(*a*) promptness of action, (*b*) suitable environment, and (*c*) psycho-therapeutic measures.

Promptness of action. Where by the use of moral
suasion, in which he should have been trained,
the Regimental Medical Officer is unable to effect
a cure at his Aid Post (this is often possible,
even sometimes in apparently severe shock), the
patient should be immediately evacuated direct
to a receiving 'centre' within the Army Area for
cases of 'shell shock', under the care there of
experienced Medical Officers. There can be no
question that this is the proper procedure, having
regard to (i) the contagiousness of the affection
within a unit, if 'shell shock' became recognized
as an easy means of escape to the Base, (ii) the
difficulty of determining to what extent the apparent mental disturbance is due to no fault of
the soldier, (iii) the undoubted fact that the disorder is very apt to become 'systematized', and
hence more difficult to cure, by the postponement
or the neglect of treatment which must inevitably
arise if such cases are admitted through the usual
channels of the general medical wards of Casualty
Clearing, Stationary or General Hospitals, where
they will be attended by Medical Officers who
have not the requisite experience, interest or
leisure to treat the affection properly.

Suitable environment. The receiving 'centre'
to which cases of 'shell shock' that require systematic treatment are first sent should be as remote

from the scenes of warfare as is compatible with the preservation of the mental 'atmosphere' of the Front. It must therefore be neither within easy range of bombardment, nor at a Base whence cases are being frequently transferred to the United Kingdom. Tents are suitable for the majority of these patients. But separate accommodation is needed (i) for cases presenting or developing such serious symptoms as demand evacuation to the Base, and (ii) for cases which are under suspicion of malingering, including those which are deemed to require disciplinary measures, such as rigid isolation, restriction of diet, etc., evoking the successive stages of indifference, resentment, and endeavour. It should be possible to apply still severer discomfort to cases of persistent exaggeration or simulation, until they yield or, after being detected *in flagrante delicto*, are sent away for punishment.

A private room or tent is essential for the use of each Medical Officer, where he can examine cases individually and confidentially, and give them the treatment suited to their condition.

Mutatis mutandis, the above recommendations are also applicable to the special hospitals or 'neurological' sections at the Base and in the United Kingdom.

A trained neurologist is by no means necessarily the most successful physician for these cases. Valuable as is such previous training for the elimination of the rare organic cases which are erroneously diagnosed as 'shell shock', and still more valuable as is an adequate previous training in psycho-pathology and psycho-therapy, what is even more important is that the Medical Officer should possess enthusiasm, confidence, cheerfulness and tact, with wide knowledge of the failings of his fellows and an ability promptly to determine whether a policy of persuasion, analysis, intimacy, sternness or reprimand should be adopted. Only the experience of such a man can lead to the successful treatment of individual patients, the detection of the (partial or pure) malingerer and the avoidance of injustice to genuine cases; and even he will occasionally fail. The number of cases under the charge of a single Medical Officer should not exceed seventy-five.

Nursing Sisters are of the greatest value, their personality, like that of the Medical Officers, being of paramount importance.

With the adoption of these measures and of systematic treatment, every advantage will be found to attend the segregation of 'shell shock' cases. If, however, they are herded together and left to themselves, they are almost sure to go from bad to worse.

Psycho-therapeutic treatment. Between wilful cowardice, contributory negligence (i.e. want of effort against loss of self-control), and total irresponsibility for the results of the shock, every stage conditioning 'shell shock' may be found. Many cases, especially those complicated by mild neurasthenia, will be found to benefit by a few days' initial rest in bed, with careful attention to sleep, diet and evacuation of the bowels. The danger, however, must not be overlooked of leaving a patient to brood in solitude over his worries and symptoms which are thus apt to become stabilized.

The psycho-therapeutic measures adopted may be conveniently classified, according to the stage of their application, as (i) restorative, (ii) convalescent.

(i) *Restorative*. Nothing can be attempted in psycho-therapy until the attention, interest and confidence of the patient are obtained. Any attempt to treat a patient during maniacal excitement, active hallucination or unyielding apathy or stupor, save by medicinal measures, is a sheer waste of time. Recovery from a condition of mild mental confusion may be often assisted by tactful persuasion; but severe stupor may be regarded as naturally imposed in order to safeguard the patient temporarily from communication with the outer world. The result of an 'emotional trauma', it cannot be regarded as falling within the 'anxiety neuroses' or the 'conversion hysterias'.

With perseverance the persistent apathetic attitude of many patients will be found to disappear;

it often connotes some congenital weakness of intellect. With tactful management states of apparent stubbornness will also pass away; they usually betoken previous mental confusion and a tendency to revert thereto.

The guiding principles of psycho-therapeutic treatment should consist in the re-education of the patient so as to restore his self-knowledge, self-confidence and self-control. For these a judicious admixture of explanation, persuasion, and sometimes scolding, is required, as in the education of children, and, where necessary, as in amnesic cases, in the restoration of a completely normal, from a dissociated, personality.

In the milder cases of 'shell shock', unaccompanied by serious loss of memory or by severe sensory or motor troubles, the emotional disturbance may often be quickly quieted by an intimate talk, the patient being encouraged to 'confess' all his fears and worries, and induced to regard them as normal experiences in the circumstances. Care should be taken to explain to him that any mild delusions, hallucinations or other unusual mental states of which he may complain are harmless and transitory, and that they will soon disappear without danger to his future sanity. The anxiety of a patient that he will be sent to a 'lunatic asylum', or returned to the Front before he feels fit for duty there, must be suitably allayed if a speedy cure is sought. It should be the physician's ultimate aim to convince the patient that he is fit for duty; and he should not return him to it until this assurance is obtained.

The mental life of a soldier is often so simple that the cause of his emotional disturbance is at once apparent. But in some cases the real cause of the patient's condition is unknown to him; and then recourse must be had to the analysis and elucidation of previous conflicts or of the dreams or strange ideas which force themselves on his notice, and to the revival of forgotten memories, if necessary under slight hypnosis. Such analysis and revival, especially where the patient is unable or unwilling himself to make the effort of successful revival, are enormously facilitated in the hypnotic state; and inasmuch as patients suffering from 'shell shock' are extremely easy to hypnotize (no doubt the effect of the shock upon their 'personality'), the Medical Officer should make appropriate use of this valuable aid in a small proportion of the cases under his charge.

The stage of hypnosis needed for the exploration of unconscious repression or dissociation is easily reached by narrowing the patient's attention and then by suggesting to him first that he is beginning to feel more and more sleepy and ultimately that he cannot open his eyes. All that is necessary is to obtain his consent to this method of cure, to get him to fix his eyes on the physician's upheld finger, and after a few seconds to persuade him to admit that his eyelids are feeling a little heavy, then that he is feeling increasingly drowsy, and finally (and peremptorily) that his eyelids are now so heavy that he cannot raise them when he now tries to do so. It is a perfectly safe and reliable procedure to adopt, provided that it be only employed for psycho-therapeutic purposes, in particular for mental re-integration or re-synthesis of dissociated or repressed memories, and not merely for the removal of bodily 'functional' disorders by suggestion. But some initial courage is needed to overcome a certain natural prejudice against its use, the first trial of it demanding more self-mastery than the first sight of a surgical operation.

Hypnosis will succeed in such cases where many weeks of psycho-analytic 'free association' and 'conversation' in the waking state may fail. The forgotten memories may relate to recent war experiences or to long previous conflicts which (by no means in all cases) it may be thought wise to revive for therapeutic purposes. Their revival, even under hypnosis, will usually need great persuasive effort on the part of the physician in order to overcome the strength of repression (or inhibition), and may be attended with so much emotion that the patient prefers to wake from the hypnotic state rather than to attempt or continue to recall them. It is a mistake to suppose that the emotions relating to the forgotten memories must necessarily be revived in their original strength with the recall of those memories, in order to effect a cure. The patient should therefore be enjoined, when in a state of light hypnosis, that he will now be able to face the forgotten situation without undue emotion. This procedure is almost invariably successful in bringing to light the 'buried complexes', if the persuasion be strong enough. He should also be told that on waking he will be able to remember all of (or even more than) that which he has just recalled, without fear or horror. He is then ordered to wake, and is thereupon asked immediately to give once again an account of his previously forgotten memories.

Similar strong suggestion and persuasion, without (or occasionally with) the use of hypnosis, will be found to cure also many cases of mutism, aphonia, paralysis, spasmodic movement, anaesthesia, hyperaesthesia, as well as the less resistant cases of amnesia. Such exciting stimuli as ether or chloroform (in the early stages of anaesthesia) or the electrical current (applied to the affected part) are of the greatest value in long-standing and obstinate cases, where the condition has become almost a 'habit'. But sometimes, especially when forcible means are employed under an anaesthetic, violent 'hysteric' excitement is displayed before a cure can be effected. As in the permissible use of hypnotic drugs in cases of 'habitual' insomnia, such methods must be regarded as mere adjuvants or accessories to analyses and explanations and to simultaneously given suggestions of recovery. Otherwise the rough-and-ready application of a second shock (or excitement) to cure a previous 'shock' is apt to convert mutism into stuttering, or to effect only an apparent cure followed by the development of some other 'functional' disturbance. The onset of fear at the application of such stimuli, or the slightest suspicion of 'torture', at all events in early cases, and in the absence of an anaesthetic, must be most carefully avoided; the infliction of pain is only justifiable in cases of long-standing neglect or of suspected malingering. In its early stages mutism is often a relic of previous stupor and is apt to revert to that condition.

In a very small proportion of cases Jung's 'word-association' method will prove useful in putting the physician on the lines of discovery of repressed 'complexes'. But prolonged psycho-analysis along Freudian lines is only possible in cases evacuated to the United Kingdom and is only advisable in the most obviously psycho-pathic patients: the 'sexual' origin of the vast majority of 'shell shock' cases is more than doubtful.

Functional deafness usually disappears rapidly. In obstinate cases of functional deafness, lipreading will be found easy to teach; and this provides a useful means of convincing the patient that he can really hear, as the Medical Officer addressing him gradually assumes a position where he cannot be seen while conversing.

Functional blindness and blepharospasm usually disappear if counter-irritation be applied to the temples and the patient be instructed to plunge his head several times daily, with eyes open, into cold water. It is as well also to correct any error of refraction if present and if possible.

But it may be necessary to trace any of these functional disorders to their emotional origin, restoring the dissociated memories to consciousness or tracing, reviving and explaining any suggestion, e.g. an intense flash of light, which may have originally provoked the disorder.

Contractures may be reduced under an anaesthetic, but they are apt to recur on the return of consciousness. Again, the physician must be warned that it is generally useless, save in long-protracted cases, to cure such physical signs until the mental disturbance underlying them has been treated. It is dangerous under an anaesthetic to fix a limb, previously in a state of contracture, in a plaster jacket, unless adequate suggestions have been made that on removal of the jacket the limb will regain its normal mobility.

Severe headache, when associated with raised pressure of the cerebro-spinal fluid following burial by a shell, may be alleviated by lumbar puncture.

Few patients are more delighted with their recovery than those who have been successfully treated for genuine 'shell shock'. The atmosphere of unfeigned optimism which should greet the newly arrived patient cannot fail to help enormously towards his speedy recovery. It is for this reason that intractable cases and those of possible malingering should be segregated from the rest.

(ii) *Convalescent*. The process of re-education in the direction of a regain of self-confidence and of ultimate return to duty must be still further pressed when the patient has passed the stage of clinical psycho-therapeutic treatment. As soon as possible, every patient should be restored to an atmosphere of increasing military discipline, gradually passing from gentle strolls and the mildest forms of exercise to longer marches and more strenuous physical drill and 'fatigues'. Such patients need to remain under the eye of the Medical Officer who has obtained their confidence from the outset, until they are ready for some form of duty. The undue neglect or pampering which they receive from inexpert hands only invites a relapse. If allowed to drift alternately between hospital and duty, in a half-cured, unstable state, these patients are apt to enter a long and costly vicious circle of recurrent mental disorder which may sometimes, among those prone thereto, eventually assume a condition of certifiable insanity.

Hence, at the convalescent stage, 'shell shock' cases should, as far as possible, be still treated in the hospital where they have been cured. In the convalescent wards each patient should be subject to a daily time-table, definite hours being allotted to amusement, 'fatigues', reading or writing, physical drill, rest, exercise, and (if necessary) special treatment. He should have ready access to the Medical Officer in case of further worry or anxiety. This is less likely to occur if the patient is fully occupied in the process of convalescence than if he be allowed to spend most of his day moping and wandering aimlessly about. His every action must be at first prescribed for him, as he is gradually coaxed and scolded, without worry, back into some form of full military discipline.

PROGNOSIS

The prognosis in cases of 'shell shock' is generally good, the speed of the patient's progress depending mainly on the severity of the shock, the absence of congenital or acquired mental instability or of past psycho-neurosis, freedom from anxiety, and appropriate treatment.

The severest cases are generally the minority that have been buried or lifted by a shell; many of these prove extremely resistant to treatment. Indeed, in rare instances it is difficult to resist the conclusion that structural damage has been caused, similar to but less pronounced than that found in the few fatal cases of burial or lifting which have been examined *post-mortem*. The occurrence of minute haemorrhages, or of lesions of a still more microscopic character, in the cortical or subcortical cerebral regions, the basal ganglia, etc., may well retard recovery from the ensuing 'functional' disorders.

It is especially among those who have most obviously succumbed to horror, fright or worry that the mental condition affords the safest ground for prognosis. As a rule, there is little correspondence between the severity or duration of the 'higher' mental symptoms and the severity or duration of the sensory, motor or other bodily symptoms (loss or increase of sensibility, palsy, contracture, ataxia, etc.). *Ceteris paribus*, those who have sustained the least emotional shock make the quickest recovery; the shock is apt especially to affect the exceptionally young, and in them to cause the gravest disturbance of the personality.

A good mental constitution, free from previous mental 'trauma', is the surest passport to a speedy and permanent recovery.

It need hardly be said that the patient's freedom from anxiety (of unknown cause or relating, e.g. to his recent war experiences, domestic troubles, return to the firing line, or doubts as to the future of his own sanity) is an essential condition for his unretarded progress, and that any such anxieties, if detected, must be at once traced to their cause and allayed in repeated private interviews.

Relapses are not infrequent during recovery, owing to passing worry, fresh emotional shock, and especially to the lack of a suitable confidant. It is the common experience of Regimental Medical Officers that a man who has twice broken down under shell fire is useless at the Front thereafter.

The essentials of treatment consist, as has been already indicated, in psycho-therapeutic measures which should be applied with the least possible delay by Medical Officers of experience; and patients should remain under their care, so far as possible, until they are fit for duty. In a word, treatment should be directed to the recovery of memory, self-knowledge, self-confidence, and self-control, i.e. to the recovery of the normal self. Then we should hear less of those later attacks of fear, accompanied by palpitation and shortness of breath, those moods of depression during which the convalescent wonders whether life is worth living, the night terrors, the shakiness and dizziness by day (especially provoked by exercise, excitement or during noise), those pranks of

memory, those worries over unrecallable inci-
dents, and other common relics of 'shell shock'
which are too often the outcome of delayed,
neglected or erroneous treatment.

PSYCHO-PATHOLOGY

We are now ready to take a more general view of
genuine 'shell shock'. The first striking feature
is that, whether any accompanying brain lesions
be relatively gross (e.g. minute haemorrhages),
microscopic (e.g. chromatolytic changes), or
ultra-microscopic; whether they be entirely ab-
sent; whether or not the ensuing symptoms be in
part determined or maintained by toxic influences
(due, e.g., to disordered internal secretion—itself
the outcome of a sympathetic or other neurosis
after the shock)—'shell shock' must be regarded
as essentially an emotional 'trauma'. One day,
perhaps, the nature of the parallel *neural* trauma
may be clear to us. But in our ignorance we can
at present only describe and discuss 'shell shock'
in psychological terms.

We are next struck by the great diversity of disturbance which may result from such a 'trauma',
and by the different causes, origins and degrees
of the 'trauma' itself. It may be difficult or impossible to draw a definite line between sudden
and gradual 'trauma', and between the cases
presenting neurasthenic, hysteric and other temporarily 'mental' disorders. Either they shade

insensibly one into the other, or they complicate one another inextricably. Indeed, the sole function which the term 'shell shock' appears to serve is to embrace under one name these disorders, of such diverse nature, arising from the emotional stress of warfare.

Typically the immediate result of the 'trauma' is a certain loss of consciousness. But this may vary from a slight, momentary, almost imperceptible dizziness or 'clouding' to profound and lasting unconsciousness. When the 'shock' is slight, the patient may be able to 'pull himself together', or he may be readily amenable to outside suggestion to this end. When the 'shock' is severe, it may be followed by unrestrainable excitement, depression, fugal automatism, or stupor, on recovery from the graver forms of which the patient can recall none of the acts performed by him during that condition. We have no means of deciding whether in the most deeply stuporose states mental processes are completely dormant. But in the states of lighter stupor and in the states of excitement, depression and automatism just mentioned, the attention of the patient would appear to be concentrated on some narrow field, doubtless generally on the scene which produced his condition. While thus occupied, the stuporose patient lies in a more or less apathetic state, with occasional outbursts of hallucinatory delirium. At this stage, then, the normal personality is in abeyance. Even if it is capable of receiving impressions, it shows no signs of responding to them. The recent emotional experiences of the individual have the upper hand and determine his conduct: the normal has been replaced by what we may call the 'emotional' personality.

Gradually or suddenly an 'apparently normal' personality usually returns—normal save for the lack of all memory of events directly connected with the shock, normal save for the manifestation of other ('somatic') hysteric disorders indicative of mental dissociation. Now and again there occur alternations of the 'emotional' and the 'apparently normal' personalities, the return of the former being often heralded by severe headache, dizziness or by a hysteric convulsion. On its return, the 'apparently normal' personality may recall, as in a dream, the distressing experiences revived during the temporary intrusion of the 'emotional' personality. The 'emotional' personality may also return during sleep, the 'functional' disorders of mutism, paralysis, contracture, etc., being then usually in abeyance. On waking, however, the 'apparently normal' personality may have no recollection of the dream state and will at once resume his mutism, paralysis, etc.

The dissociated 'emotional' personality is thus ever ready to appear on the scene, although its opportunities become fewer in the course of time. The relation of the functional 'somatic' disorders (paralysis, spasmodic movements, anaesthesia, etc.) to the experiences suffered by the 'emotional' personality is by no means clear. They would appear to be the outward expression of this dissociated personality with its highly emotional 'complex', as it works 'subconsciously' through and beneath the 'apparently normal' personality.

The physician's aim should be to restore by suggestion (aided, if necessary, by hypnosis) the experiences of the 'emotional' personality in a chastened, controlled condition, able to be 'faced', integrated with, and thus restoring, the normal personality. He should attribute the 'functional' symptoms presented by the 'apparently normal' personality to the shock which has divorced from it certain experiences represented in the 'emotional' personality. In other words, the effect of such dissociation and repression should not be regarded as confined merely to the realm of memory, but as also involving motor and sensory loss of control and even reflex disturbances, the functional 'somatic' symptoms forming part (or being an expression) of the 'psychical' dissociation which has produced the 'apparently normal' personality.

Accordingly, the treatment to be recommended—which is particularly important and easy in early cases seen in France—consists in restoring the 'emotional' personality deprived of its pathological, distracted, uncontrolled character, and in effecting its union with the 'apparently normal' personality hitherto ignorant of the emotional experiences in question. When this re-integration has taken place, it becomes immediately obvious that the 'apparently normal' personality differed widely in physical appearance and behaviour, as well as mentally, from the completely normal personality thus at last obtained. Headaches and dreams disappear; the circulatory and digestive symptoms become normal; even the reflexes may change; and all hysteric symptoms are banished.

Sometimes, however, owing to perseveration* or to obscure causes (e.g. previous emotional 'traumata'), the functional somatic symptoms persist after the individual appears to have regained full memory and control over the forgotten experiences of his mental shock. Under these conditions, and also as a result of the want of correspondence between the severity of the somatic and psychical disturbance, it is often possible, in accordance with the practice of the 'pure' neurologist, to remove the functional disorder (e.g. to restore movement by electricity or by an anaesthetic) without reference to any dis-

* By perseveration is meant the persistence or repetition of any mental state or movement.

sociated, repressed mental experiences. But so long as the latter are not restored to the individual's memory, his mental health must be regarded as in highly unstable equilibrium, at least for some considerable time.

Nature's purpose in repressing the patient's painful experiences is obvious. They demand temporary relief like any painful region or overworked organ of the body; but protracted rest and immobility are inconsistent with a return to complete health, and any undue spoiling at the hands of Nature must be avoided.

The character of the 'somatic' disorder is determined sometimes by past experiences (e.g. previous accidents, inflammations, pains, or other disorders of movement or sensation), and sometimes by the physical conditions attending the shock (e.g. a blow on the leg by falling timber, a blaze of light across the eyes, an intolerably intense sound, etc.). Some 'somatic' disorders are due to unconscious suggestion; some may even arise from conscious suggestion, extreme suggestibility being one of the slighter disturbances in personality which may be produced by the shock. But in many cases no trace of suggestion or other such cause can be found. There remains the likelihood that certain disorders (e.g. many cases of mutism) are a survival of the stuporose or confused state into which the patient had initially fallen, and that others (e.g. certain continued gestures) are the persistent expression of the emotion which has produced his condition.

The part played by 'suggestion' is by no means clear. In the pre-war period, the hysteric was believed to suffer from a 'self-suggested idea' of paralysis, contracture, hyperaesthesia, anaesthesia or the like, and it was laid down that the signs and symptoms of hysteria must therefore be such that they can be alternatively produced by the will. But we have no evidence of the universal presence of such ideas; nor do we any longer believe that the idea of a movement must be consciously present for that movement to be performed by the will. 'Functional' nervous disorders are assignable, not to deranged volition, but to a dissociated personality and its results.

Moreover, some of the 'functional' muscular disorders observed among the war neuroses (including cases that develop after wounds or fractures, which do not strictly fall under the rubric 'shell shock') are accompanied by abolition, exaggeration, or even apparent reversal, of the limb reflexes and by loss of muscular tone and excitability, often confined to the afflicted side, by local loss of warmth (hypothermia), increased sweating (hyperidrosis), atrophic changes in the nails, bones, etc. Most of these phenomena seldom occur in the absence of contracture or paralysis, and are of late development. They may appear when the contracted or paralysed limb has received only a trivial wound or even when it has received no wound at all. It has been found that many of these phenomena can be abolished by warming the affected limb and that chloroform anaesthesia often produces an exaggeration of the reflexes and of clonus on the side affected.

It is impossible to imagine that these signs of apparently reflex origin can be produced volitionally. Consequently the associated contractures or paralyses of the limbs in such cases have been themselves ascribed (first by the distinguished French neurologist, Babinski) to reflex causes; and such cases have been discharged by him and others, uncured and with pensions, from the French Army, whereas they—and the accompanying reflex signs—could have been successfully cured, in my experience, by appropriate psycho-therapeutic measures, aided sometimes by manipulation.* Moreover, the position of the limb in obviously 'functional' contractures is not necessarily one that can be reproduced by the will, nor are the dys-synergic phenomena, persistent vomiting, or tympanites observed in some cases of 'functional' disorder similarly reproducible.

If, then, 'suggestion' plays—as it undoubtedly does—a part in 'functional' nervous disorders, its influences (as we know well from the vaso-motor

* A further discussion on these 'reflex' cases will be found in my contribution to the *Lancet* of 11 January 1919.

changes producible by hypnotic suggestion) are not limited to the voluntary nervous system. Nor is it easy to understand how, through the influence of mere suggestion, long-persisting deafness, contractures or spasmodic movements can, as they sometimes do, continue during sleep; nor how, when they cease during sleep and reappear thereafter, a fresh suggestion can be given each time on waking. It is clear, therefore, that the previously employed notion of 'suggestion' is inadequate: the concept of 'dissociation' is far more important, more profound and far-reaching. The reappearance of 'functional' symptoms on waking from sleep is due not to the renewal of suggestion but to a revival of the disordered personality and of inherent dissociated emotional expressions.

Equally insufficient is the Freudian concept of a 'conflict' of incompatible behaviour involved, say, between the acquired sentiment or 'wish' to do one's duty (or between the 'censor') and the instinctive, emotional, impulse or 'wish' to escape from a dangerous situation. Repressed 'wishes', and their outlets in bodily, sometimes symbolic, action or inaction, cannot account for more than a part of the phenomena—especially late phenomena—occurring in the psycho-neuroses of war. Conflict is not an invariable cause of these phenomena; a severe emotional 'trauma' may suffice. I recall the admittedly unique case of a soldier, pre-war a University student in Wales and already twice wounded, who, after a shell had burst behind the parapet of his trench one morning, immediately lost his speech and hearing. Failing to communicate with his corporal by gesticulation, he wrote down that he wished to be allowed, despite his condition, to 'go over the top' in the attack which his unit was to make that afternoon. The corporal obtained his Company Officer's permission for this man to do so. Mute and deaf, he went through the attack satisfactorily with his Lewis gun, but received a small shrapnel wound in the leg when the order to retire was given. By his sergeant's orders, as his leg was still bleeding when he returned to his trench, he reported to the Dressing Station whence he was sent down to a Casualty Clearing Station. All this information was confirmed in a note received by me later from the Medical Officer of the man's unit. I saw the patient eleven days afterwards when he was still mute and very deaf. In the course of our conversation, conducted in writing, he remarked: "I feel quite fit physically... I've been too long up there to look on it with any fear." Having failed to restore his speech or hearing by written persuasion, I administered an anaesthetic (ether) which he took quite quietly. It was not until he had been physically stimulated that, after exhibiting extreme excitement and violence, he could be induced to speak. On 'coming round' his first act was to seek my hand and to grasp it in gratitude: his whole appearance betokened genuine pleasure. Later he asked me if there were any danger of a relapse.

The following scheme accordingly defines the broad and fundamental position we have thus reached as regards the psycho-pathology of 'shell shock':

(*a*) emotional 'trauma',

    (i) conscious, due to extreme fright, horror or other intolerable distress,

    (ii) unconscious, after physical violence,

producing

(*b*) mental 'shock', varying from slight dizziness or 'cloudiness' to profound stupor,

leading to

(*c*) disordered personality, characterized by amnesia, fission of personality, suggestibility, etc.,

accompanied perhaps by

(*d*) hysteric ('functional') symptoms, and/or by neurasthenic ('exhaustion') symptoms, in the emotional, cognitive, volitional and autonomic systems.

Chapter IV

THE DISPOSAL OF CASES IN FRANCE

THE FIRST 'MENTAL WARD'

WHEN I was first attached to Boulogne Base, early in 1915, there was no one special hospital, either there or at any other Base, for the reception of 'shell shock' cases. The so-called 'mental' cases were housed at Boulogne along an attic floor at the top of a large building which had been recently constructed as a hotel and, before its opening, converted into a General Hospital. These were a heterogeneous group, comprising cases of (i) undoubted 'insanity', (ii) suspected epilepsy, (iii) severe 'shell shock' which, owing to temporary stupor, confusion, depression, etc., could not be safely left in ordinary medical wards without a special attendant, and (iv) men who, after committing some military offence, had been admitted for a report upon their sanity and responsibility.

After the arrival of the new British Armies in France, the patients of class (i) rapidly grew in number; they included also cases of sub-normal intelligence (even of 'mental deficiency') and former 'Asylum' patients, many of whom had only been in France for a few weeks. Those of classes (ii) and (iv) often remained for several weeks in this dismal, ill-ventilated and over-crowded 'Mental Ward' under observation. Many of those in class (iii), whose condition was due to emotional 'trauma' or to mental 'ex-haustion', improved rapidly despite their highly adverse environment, some recovering so com-pletely that they were returned to military duty at a Base without being sent to England. But it was often virtually impossible to treat the readily curable cases or to observe satisfactorily those cases which required observation.

It was obvious that much harm was being done to men of classes (ii) and (iii) by being segregated, if only for a brief period, in the same ward with the acutely demented melancholic, maniacal, delusional or suicidal patients of class (i): naturally they feared that they, too, were destined for a 'lunatic asylum'.

Moreover, during their detention in this ward, the non-bedridden patients and the 'prisoners' were wholly debarred from obtaining fresh air and exercise. I was soon able to arrange for the slighter cases (with the exception of the 'prisoners') to go daily along the sea-front for a walk under supervision.

After ineffective, less formal efforts to improve these highly unsatisfactory conditions, I sub-

mitted a written report to the Medical Direc-
torate at Boulogne in July 1915, pointing out the
present conditions, and suggesting that this
heterogeneous group of (so-called) 'mental' cases
should be accommodated in one of the newly
erected 'hutted' hospitals under the charge of an
experienced mental specialist; two separate huts
being provided, the one for men of class (i), the
other for men of classes (ii) and (iii), those of class
(iv) being accommodated in one or other of these
huts according to their mental condition. I regarded it as essential that each hut should give
access to its own small 'compound' where the
patients could obtain adequate exercise, fresh air
and amusement. After the further lapse of six
months and renewed pressure on my part, satisfactory hutted accommodation, planned by me in
conjunction with the Department of Works, was
in course of construction. But as my original
scheme was not at once approved, the wards were
erected piecemeal, with the result that the whole
was not so well designed as it would have been,
had the larger scheme been approved at the
outset.

Later in 1916, with the approval of the Deputy
Director of Medical Services, Lines of Communication, I prepared a memorandum ques-
tioning the advisability of admitting to such
Mental Wards prisoners charged with, or convicted of, an offence, whose responsibility for

their act needed determination. It seemed to me undesirable that innocent men who had mentally broken down under the strain of warfare should be closely associated with those accused, or convicted, of such offences as murder, attempted suicide, theft or desertion. I suggested that the latter, in the absence of other accommodation, might, unless obviously insane, be kept in prison at some one Base under the observation of the specialist in mental diseases attached to that Base.

LATER IMPROVEMENTS

By this time improved and enlarged Mental Wards were being provided at other Bases—Étaples, Le Tréport, Rouen, Havre, and later at Marseilles and St Omer. Ultimately, often not without considerable initial difficulty and delay, all, or nearly all, my recommendations (to be mentioned immediately) were adopted, and 'temporary' Medical Officers of the Royal Army Medical Corps, with pre-war experience in Asylum work, were found to take charge of these wards. I was also successful in obtaining from each of these Medical Officers a regular monthly return based on the form given on p. 80.

In the previous April I had received instructions from the Director of Medical Services, Lines of Communication, to visit and to report to him on the accommodation of the 'mental'

RETURN OF 'MENTAL' CASES FOR THE MONTH OF
(December 1916) (Including Suspects)

	OFFICERS	OTHER RANKS
1. Remained midnight (Nov. 30) ...		
2. Admitted during month		
(a) Direct from Front		
(b) From Lines of Communication ...		
(1) Through other Mental Wards		
(2) From Elsewhere		
3. Died during month		
4. Discharges (Transfers) during month		
(a) To Convalescent Depots or duty		
(b) To England		
(1) "D" Block Netley		
(2) Elsewhere		
(c) To Mental Wards at other Hospitals in France		
(d) To Other Wards		
5. Remaining midnight (Dec. 31) ...		

Place.........

Date.........   *Signature of M.O. in charge*

cases at the various Bases. The recommendations contained in my reports were founded on the five following principles:

(i) Separation of (*a*) the acute or 'incurably' insane from (*b*) cases of temporary mental disorder due to 'nervous exhaustion' or 'shell shock' and those showing mild or doubtful signs of mental disorder; the two wards inter-communicating, where possible, by a self-closing door openable by a railway-carriage key, for convenience and economy of administration.

(ii) Separate exercise grounds for these two classes of cases.

(iii) Provision of a Nursing Sister to be in charge of the mild and harmless cases, who should be treated rather as ordinary patients.

(iv) Provision of a small room for the Sister, and of another for the Medical Officer where he could examine and treat patients with the necessary privacy.

(v) Admission of Officer patients to a Mental Ward for Officers, only when their mental state rendered them unfit for confinement in a one-bed room of a General Hospital.

At first, however, several Administrative Medical Officers at the various Bases held the superficially reasonable view that such special accommodation was unnecessary. Even in May 1916 the Deputy Director of Medical Services, Lines of Communication, shared their view that all cases of a 'mental' kind should be evacuated forthwith to England. I pointed out that

(*a*) Soldiers charged with some offence were retained for several weeks (sometimes even for months) in a Mental Ward at the Base, pending observation as to their sanity, the holding of a Medical Board and the communication to and fro (often involving great delay) between the higher Medical Authorities, the Officers of the accused's unit, and the Adjutant-General's department. During this time, the slight and (otherwise) transient cases of mental disorder were apt to deteriorate through confinement with acute lunatics.

(*b*) Many cases sent down as 'mental' owed their depressed or stuporose condition to temporary 'nervous exhaustion' or to 'shell shock' and not infrequently had nearly or fully recovered by the time they reached a Mental Ward at the Bases; obviously such cases should not be housed in the company of 'lunatics'.

(*c*) Cases were often sent down to the Base, labelled 'mental', because they were intellectually too feeble or too deficient in self-control to stand the strain of life at the Front. These were not, in the legal or popular sense, 'insane', but from the military standpoint had to be so labelled in order to get rid of them or to save them from being shot for desertion, etc.

(*d*) A large number of cases under (*b*) and (*c*) proved very soon fit for duties at a Base; whereas, if they were sent to England, they returned sooner or later in reinforcements for the Front, where, of course, they usually broke down again.

These observations, although opposed at first by several of those engaged in Medical Administration, were supported by the experience of various Medical Officers in charge of the Mental Wards at the Bases, one of whom, for example, wrote to me: "I have had an almost entire absence of trouble or difficulty with regard to any such cases which I, personally, have sent to Base duties.... Several of my cases have been so temporary as to pass the border line from insanity to sanity while under care here, and I think that the future disposal of such and many others must be left to those who are in charge of them." Another Medical Officer wrote to me: "Many of the transient and temporary forms of mental disturbance, occurring both at the Front and at the Base, show very few symptoms when they come under observation.... Many indefinite cases, such as slightly mental deficients and psychasthenics, do quite well at the Base. So far I have had no complaints of annoyance or trouble about the cases I have sent to 'Permanent Base' or to Convalescent Depôts."

Such procedure was by no means always feasible in the case of prisoners: from the military standpoint a deserter was either 'insane' and destined for the 'mad house', or responsible and should be shot. I recall my first case of this kind —a very young soldier charged with desertion, who had been sent down to Boulogne for report on his responsibility. He was so deficient in intelligence that he did not in the least realize the seriousness of his position. My only course, I thought, was to send him home, labelled 'insane'; and the sequel was that he was returned to France with a report that no signs of 'insanity' were discoverable in him. My second case, seen at another Base, a lad also unfitted for service at the Front, I decided to treat differently. I recommended that he be punished and be sent to Base Duty. But this recommendation was not followed; he was returned to the Front from which within a few weeks he was once again sent down, after having tried to bomb his officer! In a third case, seen in Front Areas, that of an intellectually feeble, stuttering young French Canadian who had deserted, I gave the same advice, which was also rejected. Shortly afterwards, I had to return to the Front and re-examine him, as during the interval he had three times deserted!

By the middle of July 1916, I had persuaded Head-Quarters, Lines of Communication, to issue an order to their various Bases that men admitted as 'mental' cases to the Mental Wards there, whose condition, in the opinion of the Medical Officer in charge, was due to temporary 'nervous exhaustion' arising from war strain, or to 'shell shock' arising from insufficient self-control, and who were likely to recover in a short time, should, as far as possible, be kept in France for treatment and should be recommended for permanent Base duties.

Shortly afterwards, my proposal to circulate a memorandum, based on my sixteen months' experience, for the guidance of medical officers in charge of 'mental' cases in France, was approved by the Deputy Director of Medical Services, Lines of Communication. But again the old difficulties, due to ignorance and misunderstanding, occurred. When forwarding this memorandum, the Director of Medical Services, Lines of Communication, described me to General Head-Quarters, quite mistakenly, as desirous of breaking one of the regulations of the Army Medical Service which lays down that all soldiers who have suffered from insanity must be invalided. His recommendation that my memorandum should not be circulated was consequently approved, despite my consequent explanation that cases of mental disorder are not necessarily certifiably insane and that a considerable proportion of the so-called 'mental' cases occurring in this war were due to temporary causes, e.g. the strain of warfare, worry, insomnia, etc., comparable to the temporary delirium of a fever or to alcoholic intoxication.

THE UNDESIRABLE SOLDIER

Early in 1916 I was attached to a Casualty Clearing Station at St Omer, then the General Head-Quarters of the British Armies in France. This Clearing Station was receiving all 'mental' cases from the First Army, and I advised on which cases should be sent to the Mental Ward at Boulogne, which to the ordinary wards at that Base or at St Omer, which to a local Stationary Hospital for rest, and which to some form of duty.

By this time I had become much concerned with a highly unsatisfactory class of soldier who was often sent home under some pretext to the United Kingdom for discharge, only to enlist again or to lead an undisciplined life there as a civilian. This class comprised such men as chronic 'alcoholics', those who, perhaps by reason of past head injuries, sunstroke, 'shell shock', etc., were easily susceptible to the intoxicating effects of small amounts of alcohol, and those, endowed with sub-normal intelligence, who were often losing articles of equipment, falling asleep on sentry duty—too irresponsible to be trusted to carry out orders, frequently insubordinate, and generally a source of danger to their comrades at the Front. Many of these men were found to have been earning a moderate wage before they enlisted, but were quite unfitted for the Firing

Line, although capable of doing useful manual labour at a Base under adequate supervision.

I was invited by the Chief of the General Staff (whom I had met) to send him in writing my suggestion that this class of men, after due warning, should be confined within 'settlements' or 'colonies' in approved localities in France, where they would be debarred from visits to *estaminets*, be treated with tact, firmness and sympathy and be provided with sufficiently comfortable quarters and suitable recreation. With proper handling under such confinement (for a reasonable length of time, if they improved), excellent work of an appropriate kind could be obtained from them. It seemed to me unreasonable that men of this class should be allowed to escape to England, and bad for the morale of the steadier and abler men who behaved themselves properly in the trenches. But, as I had feared, the Chief of the General Staff felt unable to adopt this suggestion.

ARMY AREA RECEIVING 'CENTRES'

In May 1916, towards the close of my stay at General Head-Quarters, I had come, from my clinical experience there and elsewhere, to the conclusion that a 'centre' should be provided within each Army Area for the reception of cases of ' ? mental' disorder due to, and including those of, 'shell shock' and 'exhaustion'. At that time cases of 'shell shock' and 'exhaustion' which did not demand admission to a Mental Ward were distributed throughout the various hospitals at each Base (save, imperfectly, at Rouen); they were not seen by anyone with experience of functional nervous disorders; whether they were admitted there or (in the case of minor troubles) were sent from the Casualty Clearing Stations at the Front to the Divisional Rest Stations, they received no psycho-therapeutic treatment (suggestive, persuasive, analytic, disciplinary, etc.) which experience had shown to be the fundamental methods of cure. So far as I was able to ascertain, when they had been sent to England and returned to their unit in France after four or five months' absence, their recovery was not more stable than if they had at once received treatment in France. Indeed, I was convinced from my experience that a large proportion of 'shell shock' and '? mental' cases ought not to have been sent down to the Base but could have been returned, in far greater numbers and with far greater speed, to some form of duty if they had received *early* suitable treatment away from the Base. (I had returned to duty 31 per cent. of the so-called 'mental' cases while attached to a Casualty Clearing Station at St Omer, with a quite negligible proportion of relapses.) When they were in a Base hospital almost within sight of England, their chances of rapid recovery were very much diminished, since consciously or unconsciously they were influenced by the expectation of being sent home. Moreover, the establishment of such Army 'centres' would facilitate the distinction between truly psychotic cases and those of mental disorder arising from 'shell shock' whose condition rapidly mended with rest and suitable psycho-therapy. It was by now my opinion that such cases should be treated —according to their character—either nearer the Front (within Army Areas) or in Great Britain.

Moreover, by the establishment of a 'shell shock receiving centre' in each Army Area, men who, after committing some military crime, had been remanded for an inquiry into their responsibility could be sooner examined by the mental specialist attached to such a 'centre', and a surer and easier diagnosis would thus be possible. Fewer men would be given 'the benefit of the doubt'; and malingerers would not escape to the Base, wasting several weeks at a Reinforcement Camp before they ultimately rejoined their unit.

I had been informed that some months previously the French Army had established for one of their Armies such a 'centre' for 'functional' mental disorders, including 'shell shock', and that it had proved so successful that most of the other Armies had now each its own 'centre'. I had read a report written by two French Medical Officers in charge of patients at one of these 'centres'. "It is certain", they said, "that the mentality of the functional cases treated by us is very different from that of the same cases transferred to hospitals further from the Front. ... Recovery is rapid.... There is a maximal avoidance of the fixity of the patient's attention on his complaint.... The *exaggérateurs*, the *prolongateurs* are also more curable here.... Relapses have not occurred."

The Director-General's reply to my recommendation was that it was impossible to arrange for 'mental' (!) cases to be treated in Army Areas, and that I was to take such steps as were necessary to avoid the needless evacuation to England of cases of 'shell shock' and 'nervous exhaustion' which reached the Base hospitals. I could imagine the Adjutant-General's Department, when approached by the Director-General, rejecting my proposal with the excusable, but mistaken, rebuff, "We can't be encumbered with lunatics in Army Areas!" But ultimately, as will be seen, I succeeded in getting what was so badly needed.

RECEIVING 'CENTRES' AT THE BASES

Meanwhile I had directed attention to the undesirability of admitting 'shell shock' cases indiscriminately to *any* of the hospitals at the Bases. Complaints had been received from England about the improper special labelling of these cases, the 'neurological' section of one hospital there receiving within ten days 150 cases of 'shell shock' all erroneously bearing the special label for 'organic' neurological troubles, instead of that provided for 'functional' nervous disorders. It was clearly impossible for me to trace mistakes arising from such improper labelling and in other respects to supervise the work carried on, so long as 'shell shock' patients were scattered throughout the numerous hospitals at the Bases. At Rouen this had already been largely remedied by the admission of a considerable number of cases of 'shell shock', 'neurasthenia' and other 'functional' nervous disorders to a single hospital at that Base. Although in favour of this change, Head-Quarters, Lines of Communication, were unwilling to interfere; but I was permitted to use my influence with the Deputy Directors of Medical Services at the Bases to bring it about. By August 1916 I had achieved such a measure of success that the Director of Medical Services, Lines of Communication, agreed that the 'shell shock' cases should be received at *one* hospital in each Base, so that they could come more easily and effectively under my supervision and be treated by a suitable (resident) Medical Officer who, aided by my now considerable experience, would acquire special facility in dealing with such cases. Four months later, definite instructions were issued by him to this effect, and I helped in finding suitable Medical Officers for the Bases who had had some past training and interest in analogous work.

Moreover, by the end of 1916, to my great satisfaction, the Director-General of Medical Services had agreed to arrange for the establishment of four special centres at the rear of Army Areas for the reception of cases of 'shell shock', which would also be treated by specialists appointed to those units for this purpose. Here again I was able to help in obtaining suitable Medical Officers for this work. The excellent results of establishing these Front Area receiving 'centres' became quickly manifest in the monthly returns regularly made to me on the form which I prepared, a specimen of which is shown on p. 93. From 50 per cent., rising sometimes to even more than 90 per cent., of the monthly admissions and 'remainders' were discharged direct to duty, with a negligible proportion of relapses.

THE ABUSE OF THE TERM 'SHELL SHOCK'

Early in 1916 I had become so dissatisfied with the increasing abuse of the term 'shell shock' that I recommended, in a memorandum addressed at the end of June to the Director of Medical Services, Lines of Communication, that the term should be discarded. Towards the end of the previous year, however, instructions had been received by the Director of Medical Services,

RETURN OF 'SHELL SHOCK' CASES FOR THE MONTH OF
(December 1916)

	OFFICERS	OTHER RANKS
1. Remained midnight (Nov. 30) ...		
2. Admitted during month		
(a) Relapses, i.e. within three months after returning to duty at the Front since last attack		
(b) Other cases		
3. Died during month		
4. Discharges and Transfers during month		
(a) To Duty		
(b) To Base		
(i) As 'Mental' Patients ...		
(ii) As Patients to Ordinary Wards		
(iii) As ready for Base Duty ...		
5. Remaining midnight (Dec. 31) ...		

Remarks:

Place.........

Date.........   *Signature of M.O. in charge*

Lines of Communication, from the Army Council
that 'shell shock' and 'shell concussion' cases
should have the letter 'W' prefixed to the report
of the casualty, if it was due to the enemy: in that
case the patient would be entitled to rank as
'wounded' and to wear on his arm a 'wound

stripe'. But at the Front, Regimental Medical Officers, to whom, it would appear, these instructions had not been communicated, almost invariably declined to diagnose cases of temporary (e.g. confusional) insanity due to 'mental shock' or 'exhaustion' as 'shell shock': they labelled them 'mental' or '? mental'. And some of these Officers included under 'shell shock' cases which were merely due to fear or 'nervous' collapse and had not even been near to an exploding shell. At once too much and too little were included under the term 'shell shock'. Moreover, even cases of 'shell concussion' were usually diagnosed as 'shell shock' at the Front; and inasmuch as the diagnosis did not bear the prefix 'W', these (and genuine mental 'shell shock') cases failed to rank as battle casualties.

Accordingly, I recommended that all cases of nervous or mental disorder arising from warfare (excluding gross injuries to or organic diseases of the nervous system and the insanities occurring in civil life) should be grouped, according to their symptoms, as suffering either from (*a*) 'concussion' (cerebral or spinal) or from (*b*) 'nervous shock' (functional); and that the prefix 'W' be inserted by Regimental Medical Officers both before (*a*) and (*b*) when they considered (and they were the sole Medical Officers entitled to an opinion) that the soldier's condition deserved to rank as a battle casualty, whether it be caused by shelling, bombing or mining, or be due to 'nervous breakdown' occurring in an individual exposed to abnormal strain and believed to have previously been of normal mental stability.

I felt very strongly by now that it was not only unnecessary, but also undesirable, to send down men from the Front with the diagnosis 'shell shock'. As various Regimental Medical Officers of considerable experience had informed me, "'shell shock' is often the last word of the Regimental Medical Officer under pressure from his Commanding Officer". "We have found that in certain units the complaint became fashionable, if not catching." "It would be conducive to the good discipline of His Majesty's Army if the term 'shell shock' were abolished altogether.... Its occurrence has no relation to bursting shells.... I am excluding concussion of the brain which ought never to be returned as 'shell shock'. We have seen too many dirty sneaks go down under the term 'shell shock' to feel any great sympathy with the condition." "I have to deprecate the institution and prevalence of the word 'shell shock' which has got on the tongue of all officers and men in this unit. At all times while in the trenches men are arriving at the Aid Post, and on enquiries as to their condition the invariable answer is 'shell shock'." In a private letter an Assistant Director of Medical Services had written me: "'Shell shock' should be abolished. The men have got to know the term and will tell you quite glibly that they are suffering from 'shell shock' when really a very different description might be applied to their condition." With these views I was in hearty agreement: I also had seen too many men at Base Hospitals and at Casualty Clearing Stations boasting that they were "suffering from 'shell shock', Sir", when there was nothing appreciably amiss with them save 'funk'. I considered that if the term were changed to 'nervous shock' the number of cases would be reduced, that fewer would be disposed to boast of suffering from this disorder, and that the term would cover cases of shock not due to shelling.

My recommendation was forwarded to the Director-General of Medical Services at General Head-Quarters; but his, no doubt inevitable, reaction thereupon was merely to circulate to the Medical Directors in the various Armies the previous instructions of the Army Council, retaining the term 'shell shock' and ordering the letter 'W' ('wound' class) to be affixed to all such cases (and to those of 'shell concussion') sent back by Medical Officers of Units, Field Ambulances and Casualty Clearing Stations, which were due to battle casualty, and the letter 'S' ('sick' class) to cases not due thereto.

The result of this order was that serious cases of 'shell shock' which demanded evacuation to the Base and to England were often kept in the Army receiving 'centres' for a needlessly long and (to them) anxious time until information had been received from the units to which they belonged whether their label should bear the affix 'W' or 'S'. During this interval they were, in accordance with subsequent instructions from the Director-General of Medical Services, labelled 'N.Y.D. ?N.' (not yet diagnosed, ? Nervousness), or 'N.Y.D. ? Shell-shock'; and in times of stress and consequent need for rapid evacuation they were transferred to the Bases, still bearing a 'N.Y.D.' label and still awaiting the information needed from their regiment.

It proved impossible by this means to legislate for the bad, without doing injustice to the good, soldier. I recall, for instance, a gallant artillery officer who, to his indignation, had reached one of the Bases (Havre) labelled 'Nervousness' (by which was meant 'shell shock S'). Some weeks previously, the gun emplacements of his battery had been severely shelled, a sergeant had been killed and two of his men taken to the Field Ambulance and sent down the Line marked 'shell shock W', because their mental condition originated (according to regulations) "immediately on their exposure to the effects of a specific explosion due to enemy action". But this officer whom I saw at Havre had refused to 'go sick', despite a ruptured tympanic membrane. Knowing that his battery was about to go into 'rest' behind the Front Line for some weeks, he thought that he could there manage to 'pull himself together', although at the time he felt thoroughly 'done in'. On his return from 'rest', however, the first shell that came over from the enemy, although not exploding in his immediate neighbourhood, produced an immediate recurrence of his previously disordered condition, and he was forced to go to the Field Ambulance, from which he found his way to the Base Hospital where I saw him. Whereas his two men, by giving way immediately, became entitled to rank as wounded and to wear a 'wound stripe', he; by bravely refusing to do so, was sent down later stigmatized as 'nervous'.

At the end of 1916 the Director of Medical Services of one of the Armies decided to forbid the use of the term 'shell shock' at any Casualty Clearing Station within his Area, until the patient had been investigated in the special receiving 'centre' at the rear of that Area. If, however, the diagnosis of 'shell shock' had already been made at a Field Ambulance, it was not to be altered until after inquiry and investigation of the case at the special 'centre' by the expert there. In place of 'shell shock' the terms 'shell concussion' and 'nervous shock' (as recommended by me) were to be used at the Front, cases of the former always being returned as 'wounded' and being

limited to those showing actual signs and symptoms of severe cerebral or spinal concussion
caused by a specific shell or other explosion, and
cases of the latter comprising those unable to
stand shell fire from any other cause. The latter
would always be returned as 'sick' until the final
diagnosis of 'shell shock W (or S)' had been
made at the special receiving 'centre'. It was
henceforth the duty of the Medical Officer at the
special receiving 'centre' to communicate directly
with the Officer commanding the unit to which
his patients belonged, in order to ascertain
whether any disciplinary action was contem-
plated (in which case the Officer or man would be
discharged to duty), or whether the condition
originated immediately from exposure of the
patient to the effects of a specific explosion, in
which case the diagnosis would be 'shell concussion' or 'shell shock W'. At the invitation of
this Director of Medical Services, I made a few
minor criticisms of these instructions; but they
appeared to me an excellent attempt to grapple
with one of the most serious and most difficult
problems of the war, viz. to separate the blame-
worthy weaklings from the rest.

In February 1917 further instructions were
issued from General Head-Quarters, retaining
the term 'shell shock wounded' in the case of
soldiers in whom there was evidence of direct
contact with the effects of explosion (e.g. having

been buried or blown up) and abolishing the term 'shell shock sick', patients in this category henceforth being labelled 'neurasthenia', 'hysteria' or in such other manner, according to the official nomenclature of diseases, as would meet their condition.

At the same time instructions were issued that when soldiers who had recovered at the special 'centres' established in Army Areas or at any hospital at the Base and were returned to their units, a recommendation should be sent to the Commanding Officers of such units that employment should be given them for one month on regimental 'fatigues' before their return to full duties.

Finally, a special form was issued by the Adjutant-General in June 1917 to be filled in at the special 'centres' at the rear of each Army, describing the soldier's condition and stating the supposed cause of it, and to be despatched to his Commanding Officer for him to certify, when he could do so, that the soldier had been subjected to exceptional exposure. No diagnosis beyond 'N.Y.D.N.' was to be made by Regimental or other Medical Officers who treated the case before its reception at one of the special 'centres'. In only the special 'centre' was the diagnosis 'shell shock' permissible. Instructions were also issued in regard to the disposal of this form by the Commanding Officer, if he were satisfied that the soldier had not been subjected to a specific shell explosion or to other extraordinary exposure. A copy of this form was to be attached to all medical documents accompanying the patient on his transfer to a Base hospital or thence to the United Kingdom. A patient presenting minor symptoms and fit for duty before the return of the form could be returned to his unit before the receipt of the form from the Officer commanding that unit.

Thus, after more than twelve months of un-remitting effort, despite persistent opposition and even misrepresentation of my views, I saw my main recommendations put into effect—the (virtual) abolition of the term 'shell shock'*; the provision of special receiving 'centres' both in Army Areas and at the Bases, and of an expert Medical Officer at each of these 'centres' and in each Mental Ward for the appropriate treatment and disposal of all 'nervous' and 'mental' patients and for the separation of the 'sheep' from the 'goats'. No doubt the increasing number of such patients and the obvious need for preventive disciplinary measures played a part in changing the views of the Adjutant-General and of the Director-General of Medical Services.

* In 1918, even the category 'shell shock W' was abolished in France: a soldier could only be placed in it when recom-mended by a Neurological Board at a special 'centre' in the United Kingdom.

METHODS ADOPTED IN THE
FRENCH ARMY

Strong support was also afforded to these welcome changes by the results of a visit which I was permitted to pay in the summer of 1917 to various so-called 'neurological' and 'neuro-psychiatric' centres in the French Army. In my report to the Director-General of Medical Services on this visit, I described how each of the French Armies was provided with its own 'neurological centre', consisting of about 200 beds, situated about fifteen miles from the Front Line, to which cases were admitted from the *hôpitals de triage* (sorting hospitals) within eight hours after the onset of the symptoms. These centres received all 'neurological' cases save those arising from visible wounds and were treated by Medical Officers attending solely to them, each having about 100 patients under his charge. They had been established at the instance of certain 'neurological' specialists, with the main object of reducing the number of cases of finally intractable 'nervous disorder' which had previously escaped into the 'intérieur', but which could have been at once cured by immediate attention within Front Areas. In the British Army, on the other hand, some of such corresponding special 'centres' as existed at that time were situated at a distance from the Front Line which involved far greater retardation in admission. Several hundred cases might be under the charge of a single Officer.

Whereas in the French Army few cases were evacuated from these 'centres' to the 'regional centres' of the 'intérieur', in the British Army a much larger number were then being transferred to the Bases, and a considerable proportion of these were being evacuated thence to the United Kingdom.

At these French 'centres', Nursing Sisters were not always provided, and a somewhat dreary atmosphere prevailed. There appeared to be excessive recourse to complete isolation of the patient and to the employment of the electric battery for curing cases of hysteric aphonia, mutism, paralysis, etc., the alleged abuse of which had evoked press and parliamentary protest in France owing to complaints of the 'torture' of the practice. There was insufficient provision of physical exercise and mental recreation, to which the more genuine cases were entitled. Whereas this system aimed at rather too brusque a cure (and one, in my experience, less likely to be permanent), under conditions too harsh and strict for the *severer* cases, our own methods, on the contrary, at that time inclined to too slow a cure in an environment too pleasant and too inviting for the slighter cases, and often too crowded for the patients to receive the individual attention they required.

At the French 'centres' use was made of the authority given to the chief Medical Officer to discharge suitable patients, after cure, on a week's leave of absence. This measure was regarded as a valuable incentive to recovery, as an excellent method of after-treatment, and as effecting great economy in the speed of return to duty. It might be considered hardly practicable in the British Armies in France, from the hospitals of which a soldier must first be evacuated to a hospital in the United Kingdom, where he was generally lost to France for several months.

Behind the French 'centres' at the Front, each of the '*régions*' (a term corresponding both to one of our Bases in France and to a County in the United Kingdom) had its regional 'neurological centre', under the charge of whole-time medical specialists, which received cases of a more intractable nature and organic cases from the Front, as well as the 'functional' (e.g. post-traumatic) cases arising in the rear of Army Areas. The British Bases, besides receiving cases which had resisted cure in Army Areas, were at that time receiving a variable number of 'N.Y.D.N.' cases direct from the Front, which should have passed through the special 'centres', and occasional batches of patients from the special 'centres' evacuated merely owing to pressure on accommodation.

Each of the French Armies was also provided

with a distinct 'psychiatric centre' which might
be situated in a spot remote from the 'neurological centre'. This served for the reception of
'mental' cases; but the distance between the two
centres seemed to me disadvantageous, since the
two classes of cases merged into and sometimes
complicated one another. At the British Front
no uniform provision was at that time made for
the reception of '? mental' cases; in certain
Armies they were generally sent to the Medical
Officers in charge of the Special Army Area
'centre' for examination and report.

I found that Conferences were periodically
arranged between the Medical Officers engaged
in the French 'Army' and 'Regional' neurological 'centres', for the discussion of problems
arising in their work and for co-ordinated and
uniform action. No corresponding facilities were
at that time provided for an interchange of views
between the 'neurological' or 'mental' specialists
in the British Armies in France.

The result of my visit was a recommendation
by me to the Director-General of Medical Services that, in addition, a forward 'sorting centre'
for 'shell shock' cases should be established
in each Army Area not farther from the Front
than Army Head-Quarters, each accommodating
about 250 of 'N.Y.D.N.' cases received direct
from Field Ambulances; and that a Specialist,
assisted by another Medical Officer, should be

in charge of each such 'centre'. In these 'sorting centres', the strictest attention should be paid to military discipline, to which the patients should be returned as soon as possible. No cases should be retained except those which, in the opinion of the specialist in charge, were likely to be cured within two or three days and to be fit for the Front Line after a further few days' 're-education', the severer or more obstinate cases being sent down at once to one of the Special Army 'centres' in the rear. The latter, I recommended, should also receive all doubtfully 'mental' cases for observation and report, and should be empowered to send suitable 'non-mental' cases for immediate employment on Base duty and, if possible, to the United Kingdom on short leave. (Hitherto cases cured at a Special Army 'centre' could not be sent direct to Base duty, if the hospital were situated within the Front Area, without transfer to a Base hospital, where, under a strange Medical Officer, there was a temptation for the patient to relapse.) Not more than seventy-five cases in the stage of active treatment in the Special Hospitals should be under the care of a single Medical Officer, and a clerk should be allotted to him to assist in the heavy clerical work which the existing regulations required. Only in exceptional circumstances should cases of purely 'functional' disorder or 'nervousness', uncomplicated by serious mental symptoms or by signs of organic disturbance, be evacuated from the Special Army 'centres', as patients, to the Base. I also recommended the holding of periodical Conferences of the Specialist Medical Officers concerned in the treatment of these cases.* I had previously recommended the occasional interchange of duties between these Officers in France and in the United Kingdom, in order to gain fuller experience and to improve the training courses at home.

Early in 1917, with the approval of the Director of Medical Services of one of the British Armies in France, such an Advanced Sorting Centre had been experimentally established at my request, from which a large number of cases were returned to duty after a few days' stay. This trial lasted long enough to convince me that a still larger proportion of the 'shell shock' cases at that time being evacuated from Front Areas could be cured by more immediate attention and by the maintenance of the strictest discipline, which was inevitably lost by transfer farther away from the Front Line. But this Sorting Centre was soon abolished by instructions from General Head-Quarters.

* One was held a few months after this recommendation had been made.

DEPARTURE FROM FRANCE

By now I felt that I had, under the by no means favourable conditions for some time prevailing, accomplished all that I was likely to perform in the direction of improving the treatment and disposal of 'shell shock' cases in France. When on leave, I had visited D Block (for cases of 'insanity') and the 'neurological' section (for 'shell shock' cases) at the Royal Victoria Hospital, Netley, the 'neurological' section of the 4th London General Hospital, and the Moss Side Hospital at Maghull, near Liverpool (also receiving 'shell shock' cases); thereby facilitating the co-ordination of work in the United Kingdom and in France, and the arrangements for the more effective interchange of notes bearing on the history and progress of the patients before and after arrival in the United Kingdom. In this I was also helped by the occasional visits to France of Col. Turner and of other 'neurological' and 'psychiatric' specialists from the United Kingdom, Canada and elsewhere.

I had had to deal, chiefly in the early stages of my work, with complaints made by certain patients on their arrival in England concerning alleged rough usage and unsatisfactory accommodation to which they claimed that they had been subject in France. There were also other complaints from patients suffering from 'functional' paralysis, who asserted that they had been 'tortured' by the neurologist's injudicious use of electricity or worried by other unwise treatment in France. I had seen and treated thousands of cases, and I had helped to prevent the needless transfer of a large proportion of them to the United Kingdom.

On and after the formation of the various special Army Area 'centres', I had paid periodic visits to them, sometimes of several days', or even of a fortnight's, duration, urging and demonstrating the adoption of those psycho-therapeutic measures which have since been recognized to be among the most effective methods of treatment. I had given evidence on numerous Court-martial cases and had sat on many Medical Boards. This varied work had entailed travelling many thousands of miles over roads good, indifferent and vile, in all kinds of weather, from Bases to Field Ambulances over an area of some 5000 square miles.

In the middle of October 1917, as I have already said (page 22), I was summoned to a Conference in London, over which Sir Alfred Keogh, Director-General of Medical Services at the War Office, presided, concerning the treatment of cases of 'functional' nervous disorder in the United Kingdom. This resulted later in my permanent recall, at my request, for duty in Great Britain.

I had previously explained to Sir Arthur Sloggett the personal reasons (into which it is needless to enter here) for my wishing to be relieved of my work in France. When I paid him a farewell visit at General Head-Quarters, I had an opportunity of thanking him for the courtesy and the many acts of kindness which I had received from him while serving under his command. Sir Arthur was a man of great courage and rollicking geniality, with a wide knowledge of the world, by no means an expert in any branch of medical science, but endowed with an unusual facility for choosing the most competent Officers available, with special scientific or administrative ability, for the most important work, namely in Army Areas. I found him extremely sympathetic and understanding on the occasion of this visit and generous in his estimate of my work, but evidently unwilling to take official notice of the prime causes of my dissatisfaction.

After all, I thought, as indeed a well-known General whom I left behind in France wrote to me a little later—"what do official worries and obstructed or unappreciated work count alongside of the welfare and companionship of home" after a stay of more than three years abroad?

Chapter V

THE DISPOSAL OF CASES IN THE UNITED KINGDOM

THE CONFERENCE AND THE REPORT OF ITS COMMITTEE

THE Conference held at the War Office, and the meetings of the Committee appointed by it, which I had attended from 15 October until 23 October 1917, in London, indicated a considerable amount of dissatisfaction among medical specialists with the disposal and treatment of 'neurasthenic' and 'shell shocked' soldiers in the United Kingdom at that time. In this dissatisfaction Col. Turner shared, as he had informed me before I left France. The accommodation at the Special Hospitals and of the 'neurological' sections of General Hospitals which had been set aside in the United Kingdom for these cases was obviously insufficient; the work of the Clearing Hospitals in London which received cases on their arrival from overseas was, it was alleged, being unsatisfactorily performed; and large numbers of cases were finding their way into the General and Auxiliary Hospitals throughout the United Kingdom where proper treatment was impossible, and in consequence were being invalided out of the Army uncured, totally unfit for civilian employment and enjoying a needless pension. The number of Medical Officers qualified to treat cases of 'functional' nervous disorder was also quite inadequate: they were, consequently, placed in charge of far too many cases to carry out their duties properly; and they were frequently serving under a Commanding Officer who had no knowledge of, interest in, or sympathy with their work. There was a similar lack of provision of suitable and adequately trained Nurses; and there was no permanence in the recommendations of the expert Medical Officers in regard to the disposal of their patients, e.g. whether they should be discharged from the Army or be permanently protected from return to duty overseas.

It was not surprising, therefore, that 'the wilder spirits' in this country, as Sir Alfred Keogh had described them to me (cf. p. 23), and even others more sober-minded, were now in favour of the establishment by the War Office of a 'Shell Shock' Committee which should have complete control over the disposal and treatment of cases of 'functional' nervous disorder and of the special 'neurological' hospitals to which these cases should be admitted, in the United Kingdom. This obviously unacceptable proposal was re-

jected by the Committee which, under the chair-
manship of Col. Turner, had been appointed at
the Conference.

In the report of this Committee to the
Director-General of Medical Services the need
for immediate and fundamental improvements
was clearly recognized. The Committee recommended the abolition of the Central Clearing
Hospitals in London, so that cases might be
transferred directly from the Bases overseas to
the special 'neurological centres' where they
would, without loss of time, come under the
uninterrupted care of the expert Medical Officer
who would treat them until they should become
fit for some form of military duty or for discharge
to civil employment. But the Director-General
of Medical Services, who met the Committee on
7 November, and approved of the rest of its
proposals, pointed out that owing to difficulties
of transportation Clearing Hospitals in London
must be retained, but that generally patients
would henceforth be admitted directly from overseas to the Special Hospitals and that, when
admitted to the Clearing Hospitals, they would
be transferred rapidly to the Special Hospitals.

The Committee also recommended the establishment of several additional Special Hospitals
throughout the various Commands, each of
which would contain from 250 to 500 beds, be
commanded by an Officer who had special know-

ledge of the war neuroses, and be provided with ample grounds of not less than 4 acres per fifty patients and with other facilities for employment and re-education. In the opinion of the Committee, no Medical Officer should have charge of more than fifty patients. To these hospitals the General and Auxiliary Hospitals should be instructed to transfer any cases of 'functional' nervous disorder, save those requiring special medical or surgical treatment, which might be admitted there. The Committee urged that the Invaliding Board at each such hospital should consist solely of its own Medical Officers and that the Board's decisions should be subsequently altered only with its approval or with the approval of the Board of some other such hospital. Finally, the Committee recommended that several of these 'neurological' hospitals should serve as training 'centres' for junior Medical Officers; the Military Hospital at Maghull, near Liverpool, which, under the inspiration of (the late) Major R. G. Rows, had already done admirable work both in treatment and instruction, constituting the first training 'centre' for this purpose.

MY NEW APPOINTMENTS

To this hospital, at my request, I was posted on 27 November 1917, being charged by the Director-General of Medical Services with the duty of "supervising and generally co-ordinating the psychological teaching and training of special Medical Officers in the 'neurological centres' which are about to be established in various parts of the country". Pending the establishment of these 'centres', I was asked to give Major Rows any assistance which he might desire in his next course of training which was to begin immediately.

Early in February 1918 Col. Turner informed me that, because of my past experience, he would like me to assist him in his increasing work. When subsequently I had an interview on the subject with the Director-General of Medical Services, Sir Alfred Keogh, the latter made the rather different proposal that I should be attached to his Staff at the War Office as Inspector of 'neurological' hospitals. But not unnaturally Col. Turner raised objections to this, preferring that I be attached to *him* to visit the special hospitals and to advise and report to him on treatment, etc., there. He wished me, if possible, also to join the visiting staff of the Special Hospital for Officers at Palace Green; but, because of the pressure of other work and because of my wish to be in a position to criticize freely, at that hospital in particular, I informed its Chairman (the late Lord Knutsford) of my inability to do so. A compromise was effected at a further interview with the Director-General of Medical Services, as a result of which, in the middle of February, I was appointed as an Inspector "for special duty under the War Office" and also to work "under Col. Turner, Consultant in Neurology".

FURTHER MEETINGS AND RESULTS
OF THE CONFERENCE

At this moment, Sir Alfred Keogh's appointment as Director-General of Medical Services came to an end. This was a severe blow to me, as I had gained his confidence and received much kindness from him. He was a man endowed with rare wisdom and with remarkable gifts of forcefulness and organization. I recall that he once said to me "You can always split the doctors"; and I have little doubt that on appropriate occasions during the war he exploited this maxim to the Army's advantage! Opportunity was at once taken of his retirement by members of the Conference of the previous October and by a few others, who, dissatisfied with the results of their efforts at reform, resolved to meet again and to draw the attention of the new Director-General of Medical Services, Sir Thomas Goodwin, to the report which his predecessor had generally accepted. The invitation, dated 23 February 1918, to attend this meeting, arranged for the end of February, unfortunately did not reach me until 2 March. But I attended the adjourned meeting on 12 March, at which consideration was resumed of the relations arising between the Senior Medical Officer in charge of the 'shell shock' patients and the Commanding Officer (i.e. the Asylum* Superintendent) in the case of the new 'neurological' units occupying certain Asylum buildings which were about to be taken over by the War Office from the Board of Control. The Conference, over which the late Captain (afterwards Sir) Maurice Craig presided, who was then in close touch with the War Office, urged that the duties of such a Commanding Officer should be purely administrative, and that the professional duties of his Medical Staff should include disciplinary control, the granting of leave and discharge—all of which were to be regarded as forming an essential part of the treatment of patients suffering from 'functional' nervous disorders. The Conference resolved that similar relations should hold between the Senior Medical Officer in charge of a 'neurological' section of a General Hospital and the Commanding Officer of that hospital: the Medical Officers in such a section should not be treated by the Commanding Officers as if they were attached to ordinary medical and surgical wards—two such Officers had recently been ordered to give anaesthetics; nor—as in another case—should they be warned for service overseas without the approval of their Senior Medical Officer. The Conference was further of the unanimous opinion that, when an

* The term 'Mental Hospital' has now replaced the former term '(Lunatic) Asylum'.

Asylum had to be taken over for 'shell shock' patients, every effort should be made to obliterate any characteristically Asylum features; and that, with this object, the nursing of these patients should be carried out not by the Asylum nursing staff, but by specially selected Sisters assisted by probationers mainly of good education, in the choice of whom the Senior Medical Officer should have wide powers.

Inevitably my position in accepting the invitation to attend these meetings of the Conference soon became difficult. On the one hand, its deliberations might be regarded at least as a safety-valve for 'letting off steam', or at best as suggesting new improvements and as affording support for 'getting things through' by periodic meetings of the Conference with the Director-General of Medical Services. On the other hand, the Conference might be regarded as an un-authorized, self-constituted and unrepresentative body, often interfering needlessly or even dangerously through its ignorance of administrative and other difficulties. Like myself in the earlier days of the Conference, Col. Turner wavered for some time between these opposite views; but finally he empowered me to inform the Conference that he shared my favourable opinion as to the value of its work, and that he would be willing to attend future meetings if he were not expected to sign any document. I had of late been urging either that Col. Turner should be invited by the Conference to its meetings, or else that it should at once seek an interview with the new Director-General of Medical Services in order to acquaint him with its members' views and to have the Conference officially recognized. I felt convinced that the former course would conduce to the happiest results and to the successful achievements of the various reforms advocated by the Conference, for nearly all of which no member of it, I pointed out, was more anxious than I.

As an initial step towards meeting the resolutions of the October Conference, I was able to arrange with Col. Turner (*a*) that one-quarter of the bed accommodation available at the special 'neurological centres' in five of the Commands throughout Great Britain be in future reserved for cases coming directly from overseas and not passing through the London Clearing Hospitals, and (*b*) that Army Medical Officers engaged on permanent home duty be asked to volunteer for service in these special 'centres' for 'functional' nervous disorders. The visits which by now I had begun to pay to these 'centres' throughout the country had already revealed to me not only the shortage of Medical Officers but also the lack of knowledge of many occupied in the treatment of the cases. For example, in a well-known, formerly civilian, hospital taken over by the Army, I found a Medical Officer who, after being invalided from France, had been sent there to take charge of 'shell shock' and 'neurasthenic' patients without demand, interest or previous experience. He told me that he was longing to treat certain other medical cases. He had had as many as 130 cases under his charge; and he confessed to me that, even if he had the time, he had not the knowledge how to treat his cases. In another smaller hospital, the resident Medical Officer who had had sixteen years' Asylum experience and had been wounded in France, told me that many of his patients had already been in six different hospitals before admission and that he 'Board'-ed about 80 per cent. of them for discharge from the Army. He said that he took no interest in the psycho-neuroses and would far rather be employed in Asylum work. In a third hospital—for diseases and injuries of the nervous system in peace-time—I found a Medical Officer whose interest lay, he said, in 'organic' cases only and who was treating cases of war neurosis only because he was compelled to do so. Many of his patients, who had likewise been previously in several hospitals, were suffering from long-standing 'functional' contracture or paralysis (including mutism): these he cured by persuasion or by mild application of electricity and on recovery invariably recommended their discharge from the Army. For him hysteria was limited to 'functional' motor disorders; 'functional' sensory disorders he ascribed to malingering; and the dissociations revealed by amnesia and other mental disturbances were not in this hospital regarded as part of hysteria: they did not occur, he maintained, in hysteric women! He knew nothing, he said, of psychology and classed all psychical disturbances as 'mental' or as 'neurasthenic'; these, he confessed, he did not know how to treat, nor had he the time to do so!

Orders were at this time framed (*a*) that all matters involving a personal and medical knowledge of the patients in such hospitals (including their leave and 'Board'-ing) should be among the duties of the Senior Medical Officer in charge in consultation with his Commanding Officer, and (*b*) that the Senior Medical Officer, or the Medical Officer in charge of the patient, should also be consulted by the Commanding Officer of the Hospital when breaches of discipline had to be considered or when work for the convalescent in the grounds or shops of the 'centre' had to be prescribed.

At the next Conference, held on 4 April 1918, it was agreed that Medical Officers who wished to undertake work on the war neuroses be instructed to report directly to Col. Turner and that no Medical Officer already qualified for such work should be sent overseas, unless in response for services in 'neurological' units abroad.

DEFECTS AND REMEDIES

Col. Turner agreed with my proposal to establish training 'centres' in the London district and elsewhere, to ask for monthly returns of 'neurasthenic', 'shell shock' and 'mental' cases arriving in London from overseas, and to arrange that from each Command in the United Kingdom returns of fresh cases arriving there be reported to the nearest special 'centres' for admission. He also undertook to ascertain how such cases might be later traced if at the time of their arrival in the different Commands no accommodation was available in the special 'centres'. Again I stressed the need for obtaining additional Medical Officers and additional beds in these 'centres': in one Command, for instance, 1000 cases were reported to me, with only 300 special beds provided.

I further urged the abolition of the small subsidiary 'centres' which I had found to be doing unsatisfactory work throughout the various Commands. In several of these I had met with many cases of 'functional' nervous disorders which had been there, or in a series of General or Auxiliary Hospitals, for from six to twelve or more months. Some were objectionably near to Mental Asylums. I recall one large country house, with no resident Medical Officer, containing fifty beds, which was visited once weekly by the specialist in charge of the 'neurological centre' seven miles away; but he was occupied during these visits almost wholly in 'Board'-ing the patients there. There was no time for him to give attention, even in the main 'neurological centre', to cases of anxiety, disturbing dreams, etc.; this specialist pinned his faith to 'time' and 'happy surroundings' to effect a cure! In two such places an unqualified medical student and an Indian were, respectively, in charge. In others Medical Officers with Asylum experience were in charge, treating their patients, as might be expected, usually by rest, bromides and other hypnotics; in others, on the contrary, the practice of the 'pure' neurologist prevailed—the application of massage and electricity (sometimes only by Nurses), splints and isolation. Little or no outdoor exercise or occupational work was usually provided, and often scant discipline was maintained; in some 'ergotherapy' was employed prematurely, with bad results; a dour atmosphere frequently prevailed; and in several, characterized by an entire absence of psycho-therapeutic measures, 80 per cent. or more of the patients were being 'Board'-ed for discharge from the Army.

In one large 'centre', receiving mainly recent cases, patients suffering from aphonia or stammering were forbidden to speak; they were merely told that, as their condition improved, they would talk normally. Psycho-therapy was limited to assurances that these and all other patients would recover 'in time'; they were enjoined to forget all their worries and to record their dreams in a book and so familiarize themselves with them! Where the General Hospital contained a 'neurological section', there tended to be friction between the Senior Medical Officer in charge of the section and the Officer commanding the whole hospital, who had little knowledge, interest or sympathy in regard to 'functional' nervous disorders. The Clearing Hospitals both for Officers and Other Ranks were not content to sort and to clear: they retained many more cases than was compatible with the proper discharge of their functions, in order to treat them—not always, in my view, according to the best therapeutic principles. Sometimes, under favourable conditions, I gave a demonstration of the methods that should be used in the successful treatment of contractures and aphonia and of 'mental' troubles. But this was seldom possible or profitable.

It was no wonder, then, that I felt wholeheartedly sympathetic towards the consideration and removal of nearly all the unsatisfactory features brought forward by the members of the Conference at their successive meetings. I endeavoured to arrange that no cases of 'functional' nervous disorder should be 'hospitalized' for more than six months; that for the time being preference be given in the new and improving neurological 'centres' in the provinces for the admission of new cases direct from overseas; that no case of functional paralysis or contracture should be 'Board'-ed uncured until he had been seen by the 'neurological' specialist whose appointment was then being advocated for each of the Commands; and that outdoor and indoor work should be provided both for Officers and Other Ranks in the convalescent section attached to the 'neurological centre' in which they had been successfully treated.

On 24 April 1918 the Director-General of Medical Services invited four of the senior members of the Conference, with Col. Turner, to attend a discussion. The next full meeting of the Conference was held on 10 May, at which a proposal to obtain its official recognition was unanimously rejected, mainly because of the feared impairment of its freedom. It was reported that the provision of special labels was now to be abandoned for all disorders and injuries; the practice had never been carried out very satisfactorily, especially when there was considerable pressure on evacuation; and a large proportion of cases, properly labelled to a Clearing Station, had always failed to reach their destination from overseas. I insisted on the need for thirty additional Medical Officers for cases of 'functional' nervous disorder by the end of the next three months, when only twelve trained Officers would by that time be available. It was also suggested that a certain proportion of the patients about to be discharged from the special 'centres' be retained as orderlies, for which work, it appeared, they would be specially suitable. Col. Turner undertook to inquire into these two matters, subsequently, however, consenting to my action in regard to the former.

I had already insisted that 'mental', i.e. psychotic, cases should not be treated in the same 'centres' as 'neurasthenic' patients. At the next Conference, held on 13 June 1918, I was asked to arrange that epileptic patients should also not be admitted into 'neurological centres'. It was also agreed that a distinguished member of the Conference should frame a letter, approved by Col. Turner, (now) Lieut.-Col. Craig and myself, for publication, with the consent of the Director-General of Medical Services, in the medical journals, asking that medical men about to join the Royal Army Medical Corps, and interested in cases of 'neurasthenia', should send in their names to the War Office. (An announcement to this effect appeared in the *Lancet* of July 20.) Lieut.-Col. Craig undertook to endeavour to obtain specialist's extra pay for those expertly treating the war neuroses—a demand which had often been previously made of me, but which had been hitherto refused on economic grounds. The short-comings of the London Clearing Hospitals both for Officers and for Other Ranks suffering from 'functional' nervous disorders, and their inadequate staffing, were also discussed.

A REPORT TO THE DIRECTOR-GENERAL OF MEDICAL SERVICES

By the end of July I had paid over fifty visits to the thirty special 'centres', auxiliary and other hospitals which were housing 'neurological' cases in the London District and throughout the various (including the Scottish) Commands, and I had seen the Deputy Director of Medical Services or an Assistant Director of Medical Services in each. A month previously, as Inspector under the War Office, I had submitted a report of this work to the Director-General of Medical Services, pointing out that while it was undoubtedly true that some patients, suffering from neglected 'functional' contracture, paralysis and the like, regained normal control over their muscles when treated merely by electro-therapeutic measures, manipulation, or isolation (combined with mild suggestion and subsequent re-education), a large number of such patients required, in addition, special treatment of the disturbed psychical condition which had been responsible for the onset of their 'functional' bodily disorder; that all cases of purely psychical dis-

turbance (e.g. worries, fears, dreams, hallucinations, obsessions) needed detailed psychological
examination and psycho-therapy; that while the
general 'atmosphere' was most important, systematic employment should not be given to a
patient before appropriate treatment had brought
him to an advanced stage of convalescence, his
improvement being encouraged only in exceptional circumstances by the promise of discharge from military service; that consequently
all three forms of treatment, physico-, psycho-
and ergo-therapy, should be employed by every
Medical Officer in each of the special 'neurological' hospitals, the patients being selected for
these different forms of treatment according to
the nature, severity and stage of their condition.
I also recommended that when the Officer commanding such a unit was himself a specialist in
'functional' nervous disorders, he should be
relieved of the routine part of his administrative
duties by a non-specialist Adjutant attached to
his staff. I pointed out that successful treatment
depended mainly on the personal influence of the
Medical Officer under whose care the patient was
placed, and that consequently the latter must
come under the constant supervision of a *resident*
Medical Officer specially qualified for, and keenly
interested in, this particular branch of medicine
and remain under his care until recovery or
discharge. I insisted that no Medical Officer

should have charge of more than seventy (pre-
ferably fifty) patients; that a private room was
essential for each Medical Officer, where he could
confidentially interview and treat his patients;
that a Visiting Consultant was useless for purposes of treatment unless he could afford time to
spend an hour or more over a single case at each
visit as necessity demanded; that 'neurological'
patients needed to be nursed by women of good
social and educational level and should be provided with adequate grounds for exercise and
occupation, instead of being confined within
locked doors, barred windows and special airing
courts, as actually occurred when they were
accommodated in the same building with cases of
serious mental disorder. Many of these recommendations had been already considered and
approved at meetings of the Conference.

I indicated the various places where, as I had
observed, the above conditions were not fulfilled,
in spite of Col. Turner's efforts and my own, as
his Assistant, to improve them; and I referred to
the large numbers of long-standing cases awaiting
admission to the 'neurological centres' from
other hospitals in the same Command, which,
owing to neglected or improper treatment, had
now become difficult to cure and blocked the way
for the direct admission of the fresh and more
hopeful cases from overseas; to the consequently
long retention of cases in the special 'centres',

due also to the inadequate training of Medical Officers in charge of them there; and to the lack of opportunity for individual attention to them owing to the excessive number of cases under the care of each Medical Officer, or to his engagement in writing up the necessary forms for the discharge of so many patients from the Army.

FURTHER IMPROVEMENTS

It was my conviction that at least 70 per cent. of the patients admitted *directly* to the special 'neurological' hospitals in the United Kingdom should prove available for some form of military service, whereas at that time a considerably larger proportion than this was being pensioned and discharged from the Army. This was partly due to the neglect of a relevant Army Council Instruction that the patient be not sent overseas within a given period, or to the immediate disregard of the medical recommendation, on the patient's discharge from hospital, that he be employed only for military work of a special kind (e.g. garrison duty, sedentary or other specified employment which was frequently non-existent for him). Repeated instances of these practices had been brought to my notice, the result of which was that in many of the special 'centres' Medical Officers were discharging nearly every patient from the Army, finding that the 'atmosphere' of the hospital deteriorated as their patients began to lose faith in the promise made to them (in order to alleviate their anxiety and to promote their cure) that they would not be sent overseas for at least six months. Thus had also arisen a certain slackness in the rate of recovery and a tendency to the deterioration of discipline. These dangers I was able to combat by obtaining the issue, on 25 June 1918, of a further Army Council Instruction (No. 712).

As I have already stated, I was successful in securing the allocation of 25 per cent. of the vacant beds in the special 'centres' for the reception of cases transferred from the London Clearing Hospitals on their arrival from overseas, the latter hospitals being regularly informed by the Officers commanding these 'centres' as to the number of vacant beds available. I endeavoured also to arrange that every hospital should report directly to its nearest 'neurological centre' all cases of 'functional' nervous disorder (which, however, were occasionally unrecognized as such) admitted, together with the date of origin of the disorder; and that the special 'centres' should allocate 25 per cent. of their beds for the im- mediate admission of such cases which were of recent origin. But I failed to get instructions issued that no patient suffering from 'functional' paralysis or contracture should be discharged from the Army until he had been treated in a special 'neurological centre' in the United

Kingdom, or that no case of 'functional' nervous disorder should be retained in any hospital for longer than six months, save with the approval of a Command or the War Office 'Mental' Specialist. Such specialists for mental disorders had already been appointed in each Command, but I was successful in resisting the proposed appointment of corresponding 'neurological' specialists in each Command, unless it be for the detection of 'functional' cases wroιgly retained, or about to be 'Board'-ed, in General or Auxiliary Hospitals. What was sorely wanted, as I pointed out to the Director-General of Medical Services in my report, was a larger number of Medical Officers willing to be trained for work in the special 'neurological' hospitals.

COMPARISON OF MY WORK IN FRANCE AND GREAT BRITAIN

The cases which I had been seeing in England and Scotland since my return from France were not fundamentally different from those seen by me abroad. But the symptoms, owing to their long duration, had become more thoroughly systematized and stereotyped, and therefore harder to cure. And 'complexes' of pre-war origin and domestic worries were more frequent and more prominent. Moreover, there was a very much larger proportion of 'functional' contractures and paralyses of the limbs, many of which had arisen after leaving France, often after the removal of a splint following surgical treatment for a wound to the limb received there; the 'functional' nature of these cases had often remained long unrecognized. It was more difficult in this country than in France to ensure an adequate number of properly qualified Medical Officers, partly owing to the demand for their services overseas. And the hospital accommodation was more inadequate and unsuitable, the latter feature being partly due to the acceptance of inappropriate gifts of town and country houses from wealthy benefactors and to the 'influence' sometimes exerted by them, when of high social standing, in order to ensure that acceptance.

My work was even more difficult at home than it had been in France: it needed no little tact to 'hunt' with the 'wilder spirits' of the Conference and to 'run' with the making of minor changes which Col. Turner was willing or able to effect. He and I worked together, as in France, quite harmoniously. I soon felt convinced that no amount of experience and knowledge, anticipation and vision, resolution and forcefulness, exhibited by a single man, could have prevented most of the difficulties besetting the proper disposal and treatment of the cases of 'functional' nervous disorder in this country. The number of these cases had so rapidly increased, both those the incidence of which could be traced to the

Front Line and those in which the condition had developed in this country. The 'general run' of Medical Officers were so little trained in the, diagnosis and care of the psycho-neuroses that they were incompetent either to recognize or to treat these conditions. Cases accumulated un-cured also because of inevitable anxiety over a pension. And, as a broad generalization, the efficiency of administration throughout the Army Medical Service diminished from the Front Areas to the Bases, and thence to the remoter parts of England and Scotland, complicated as it often was by civilian difficulties and by other adverse influences or obstructions.

Useful as the members of the Conference had proved themselves, they were a very 'mixed bag', comprising psychiatrists, psycho-therapists, psy-chologists and 'pure' neurologists—not infre-quently 'pulling different ways' in regard to principles of treatment and (in the case of certain senior members) in regard to future leadership. In the case of two or three of them, I strongly suspected that they regarded my willingness to assist Col. Turner with my experience in his increasingly difficult work, and my participation in the meetings of the Conference, in the light of the actions of an unwanted, if not treacherous and self-seeking, interloper. As for Col. Turner, he came naturally to look with disfavour on my interviews with the Director-General's Assistant, in my position as Inspector under the War Office, and indeed ultimately he informed me that the Assistant-Director of Medical Services had ordered me only to report through himself. But this appears likely to have been a 'wishful' misunderstanding, as the official concerned assured me not long afterwards that he could never have made such a demand. The truth is that the 'nerves' of every one of us at home were 'on edge' during these anxious later years of the war.

In this country I had no longer to give evidence, as in France, on Courts-martial, endeavouring to save soldiers from being shot for desertion, etc., who were clearly not wholly responsible for their acts, or to insist on punishment from which a Mental Specialist, with long engagement in Asylum work, would not uncommonly tend to excuse a soldier because of that biased experience. I still sat on a few Medical Boards, the unsatisfactory nature of which may be illustrated by the following occurrence. In July 1918 Col. Turner asked me if I would attend every week one of the three weekly afternoon meetings of the War Office Medical Board as a specialist in regard to the disposal of 'neurasthenic' and similar cases about to be discharged from the War hospitals. I replied that I had already had experience of the procedure of this Board and was dissatisfied with it, that no doubt an oculist or aurist could give a definite opinion on the state of a soldier's eyes or ears after a few minutes' examination, and that, correspondingly, in some cases of 'nervous' or 'mental' disorder the condition was so obvious as to be apparent at first sight and indeed often without the need of expert opinion; but that the more obscure or border-line cases required from 30 to 45 minutes' examination at the hands of the specialist, which should be carried out on the morning *before* the afternoon meeting of the Board, as it was not practicable to do this when the Board was already assembled and would be waiting to proceed with other cases (which might also require the 'neurologist's' opinion). I informed Col. Turner that unless this could be arranged, I felt incompetent to offer the Board any adequate guidance. My proposed place on the Board was filled by the Mental Specialist who had been attending the other two weekly meetings.

THE ARMISTICE

My work continued to increase until, after the Armistice in November 1918, I was demobilized in the March following. During this interval the Conference continued to meet monthly or bi-monthly: it had become by now officially known as the Neurological Advisory Committee and was attended not only by Col. Turner and myself but occasionally also by one of the staff of the Director-General of Medical Services, from the War Office. For some time many additional 'neurological centres' had been opened in various parts of the country; I was also occupied in visiting them and in assisting Col. Turner to provide them with a properly trained medical staff; I helped not only to open training 'centres' in two or three places for these Officers, but also to persuade their teaching staffs to visit one another so as to learn something of each other's methods when they differed. At the same time, much unsatisfactory accommodation had been abandoned. To some extent I had succeeded in improving the disposal and treatment of the Officers received from overseas at the Clearing Hospital in London, with its annexes or subsidiary hospitals, and at another hospital which, with its annexes, also received and 'treated' Officers direct from overseas. But although the Conference generally approved of my endeavours, 'influence' sometimes stood in my way. Indeed, as war weariness and war pressure increased, my work at reform became increasingly difficult and disappointing. After the Armistice, I helped in an endeavour by the Conference to get the training 'centres' continued for the treatment of the war neuroses and allied conditions, so that the knowledge of the methods so successfully carried out in these 'centres' by the Army during the war might not lapse during the period of transition, before instruction on the subject could be taken up by the Universities or Medical Schools in civil life.

From this time the problem passed largely to the treatment of pensioned ex-Army patients who could still be accommodated in Military Hospitals. Endeavours were made, in accordance with the recommendations of the Conference, to transfer from the special 'centres' expert Army Medical Officers who wished to undertake service under the Ministry of Pensions for the diagnosis and treatment of the war neuroses; a small Committee of the Conference, held in March 1919, being formed at my suggestion, to press this procedure immediately on the Principal Medical Officer of the Ministry while such Officers' services were still available and before their return, after demobilization, to civil life.

Several hundreds of instances, occurring during the year 1918, were reported at a Conference meeting from one of the 'neurological centres', of patients whose condition had not been previously recognized as one of 'functional' nervous disorder and who were about to be 'Board'-ed out of the Army with receipt of a 60–100 per cent. pension, who were instead transferred by an expert member of the Medical Board to this 'neurological centre' and cured there. It was stressed that the arrangements for demobilization would result in the invaliding from the Army of a largely increased number of patients whose 'functional' conditions were curable but who would be awarded high pensions, instead of being cured first or of being awarded, once and for all, a definite gratuity instead of an alterable pension before they were cured, upon discharge.

The persistence of 'functional' nervous disorders in relation to the receipt of a pension was clearly illustrated by some cases reported to the Conference, e.g. that of an already discharged and pensioned soldier who had been successfully cured of his long-standing symptoms at a 'neurological centre', but had suffered a relapse as soon as he realized that he was now in danger of losing his pension. For this and similar reasons, the French Government had decided that, save in exceptional circumstances, no case of purely 'functional' nervous disorder should be entitled to a pension. But apparently our own Authorities feared to face public opinion by adopting so therapeutically valuable a measure.

MY DEMOBILIZATION

On 31 March 1919 I was demobilized, not altogether unwillingly. For I was by now tired of the many difficulties and frustrations which had beset me in my four and a half years' work. Before leaving the Army, I appealed to the

Director-General of Medical Services for some recognition on behalf of certain junior Medical Officers of the 'neurological' service who to my knowledge had done brilliant and strenuous work in a most unostentatious manner. As I pointed out, no members of the Royal Army Medical Corps had worked harder, spending the whole morning and a large part of each afternoon, year in and year out, in the wards, engaged in a task of treatment far more trying and exhausting than that of ordinary operating, fracture-setting, wound-cleaning, palpation or auscultation. But neither in France nor in the United Kingdom, so far as I was aware, had a single 'mention' or other distinction been up to that time conferred on any Medical Officer in the British Army for this work.

The Director-General of Medical Services received me with his usual courtesy and kindness. I had had little touch with him since his appointment at the War Office, as (to save him trouble) I usually consulted the appropriate junior members of his Staff there. But I had known him well in France, when in the early days of the war he commanded a large hospital at Wimereux. He was evidently familiar with my experiences in France and referred sympathetically to them. This led to conversation on more personal matters which are not suitable for mention here.

With this farewell visit ended my medical

work in the Army of the last Great War, and after leave granted by the University I returned to my psychological laboratory at Cambridge. The recall of my past five years' work proved too painful for me to accept the subsequent invitations either of the Medical Research Council to help in its historical and statistical work for the Army Council or of the War Office Committee on Shell Shock to give evidence before it. Indeed, as may be imagined, the revival of these long-repressed memories—particularly those of certain experiences which I have refrained from mentioning—has been extremely unpleasant during the preparation of this volume. But if it serves to save similar unhappiness to others, and a more rapid attainment of efficiency by the taking of 'short cuts' indicated by experience and by the avoidance of 'pitfalls' otherwise unforeseen, I shall feel more than compensated.

Glossary of Medical Terms

Amnesia: loss of memory.
Anaesthesia: loss of sensation of touch.
Analgesia: loss of sensation of pain.
Aphasia: loss of speech.
Aphonia: loss of voice.
Asthenopia: easily tired vision.
Ataxia: loss of muscular co-ordination.
Atrophy: loss of nutrition of tissue and consequent changes.
Bradycardia: abnormally slow heart-beat.
Cervical: of the neck.
Cheyne-Stokes breathing: rhythmical increase in depth of res-
    pirations to a maximum, followed by decline to a minimum,
    a complete stoppage, a rise to a maximum depth, and so on.
Clonus: a series of spasmodic muscular contractions.
Dermatographia: the persistence of marks made on the skin by
    a blunt-pointed rod or finger.
Dys-basia: an affection of the gait.
Dys-synergia: lack of normal muscular co-operation.
Epistaxis: nose-bleeding.
Fugue: a trance-like period of conduct, of which the person has
    later no memory.
Glycosuria: the presence of sugar in the urine.
Haemoglobin: the colouring matter of the red blood-corpuscles.
Hemiplegia: paralysis of one side of the body.
Hippus: rhythmically alternating dilatation and constriction of
    the pupil.
Hyperaesthesia: abnormally increased sensitivity to touch.
Hyperalgesia: abnormally increased sensitivity to pain.
Hyperidrosis: abnormally increased perspiration.
Hyperthyroidism: condition due to abnormally increased activity
    of the thyroid gland.

Hypertonus: abnormally increased muscular tone.
Hypothermia: lowered temperature of the skin surface.
Hypotonus: abnormally decreased muscular tone.
Intercostal: between the ribs.
Monophlegia: paralysis of one limb (or part of it).
Nystagmus: oscillating movements of the eye-balls.
Oedema: dropsical swelling of the tissues beneath the skin.
Paraplegia: paralysis of the lower part of the body and legs.
Paresis: incomplete paralysis of a muscle (or group of muscles).
Rombergism: unsteady stance when the eyes are closed.
Tachycardia: abnormally rapid heart-beat.
Vertigo: giddiness.

INDEX

www.ingramcontent.com/pod-product-compliance
Ingram Content Group UK Ltd.
Pitfield, Milton Keynes, MK11 3LW, UK
UKHW042145280225
455719UK00001B/116